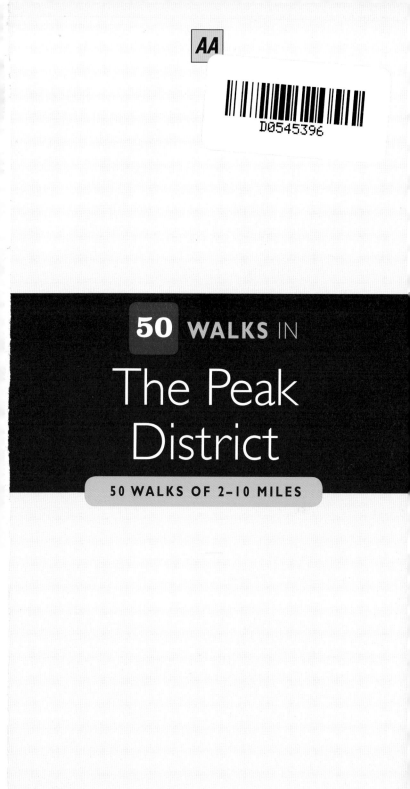

AA

D0545396

50 WALKS IN
The Peak District

50 WALKS OF 2–10 MILES

First published 2002
New edition 2008
Reprinted July 2009, February and July 2010

Researched and written by John Morrison,
Andrew McCloy, John Gillham, Hugh Taylor
and Moira McCrossan
Field-checked and updated 2007 by
Andrew McCloy

Series Management: Bookwork Creative
Associates
Series Editors: Sandy Draper and
Marilynne Lanng
Designers: Elizabeth Baldin and
Andrew Milne
Picture Research: Michelle Aylott
Proofreaders: Suzanne Juby and Pamela Stagg
Cartography provided by the Mapping
Services Department of AA Publishing

Produced by AA Publishing
© AA Media Limited 2008

Published by AA Publishing (a trading name
of AA Media Limited, whose registered office
is Fanum House, Basing View, Basingstoke,
Hampshire RG21 4EA; registered number
06112600)

A04520

ISBN: 978-0-7495-5598-6
ISBN: 978-0-7495-6403-2 (SS)

A CIP catalogue record for this book is
available from the British Library.

Colour reproduction by Keenes Group,
Andover
Printed by Printer Trento Srl, Italy

Acknowledgements
The Automobile Association would like
to thank the following photographers,
companies and picture libraries for their
assistance in the preparation of this book.

3 AA/T Mackie; 7 AA/A Tryner; 9 AA/J
Morrison; 11 AA/T Mackie; 24/25 AA/AJ
Hopkins; 41 AA/T Mackie; 42 AA/A Midgley;
70/71 AA/N Coates; 93 AA/AJ Hopkins;
94 AA/N Coates; 122/123 AA/AJ Hopkins;
139 AA/AJ Hopkins; 140 AA/AJ Hopkins;
156/157 AA/T Mackie

Right: View over Cromford from Black Rocks (Walk 45)

50 WALKS IN
The Peak District

50 WALKS OF 2–10 MILES

Contents

Contents

Rating

Each walk is rated for its relative difficulty compared to the other walks in this book. Walks marked +++ are likely to be shorter and easier with little total ascent. The hardest walks are marked +++

Walking in Safety

For advice and safety tips see page 176.

Locator Map

Legend

--⇢--	Walk Route	▨	Built-up Area
❶	Route Waypoint	▨	Woodland Area
- - - -	Adjoining Path	🛉🛉	Toilet
⚡	Viewpoint	P	Car Park
•	Place of Interest	⊞	Picnic Area
⌂	Steep Section	)(	Bridge

Right: The steep granite hills and valleys of Dovedale (Walk 42)

Introducing the
Peak District

The Peak District sits at the base of the Pennines, with one foot in the North and one in the Midlands. At its northern tip, the high moorlands merge seemlessly into the South Pennine massif dividing Yorkshire and Lancashire. In the south the graceful River Dove sparkles out of the limestone landscape, dividing Derbyshire and Staffordshire. Between these two contrasting images lies the Peak District National Park, a backyard playground for the city dwellers of the East and North Midlands, South and West Yorkshire and Greater Manchester. Surely nowhere else in Britain offers so great a contrast in landscapes, to so many people, in such a relatively small area. The Peak District National Park was the first National Park to be established in England (in 1951) and protects 542 square miles (1,404sq km) of this precious environment.

Plateau

But you shouldn't expect to find any mountain peaks in this beautiful upland. The name comes from the Old English 'peac' which describes a knoll or hill. With a few notable exceptions, the heights are predominantly plateau-like, carved with deep valleys which give a sense of elevation to the various edges and occasional summits bold enough to lift their contours above the rest. Best-loved among these are the conical elevations of Shutlingsloe, Shining Tor, Chrome Hill and Parkhouse Hill and you can be forgiven for assuming that the region took its name from their magnificent pointed crests.

Dark Peak

The northern area is known as the Dark Peak. It's one of brooding moorlands, green valleys and many reservoirs. From the gritstone outcrops and peaty morasses tumble well-fed streams. The abundance of water drew the industrialists of the surrounding conurbations and virtually all the valleys except Edale boast a reservoir, or often several. You'll see this as you walk around the moorland fringes of West and South Yorkshire, in the Holme Valley and around Bradfield. From Glossop, Hayfield, Longdendale and Chinley on the western side each valley seems to have been dammed in turn. The most dramatic is the upper Derwent Valley, where villages were removed and vast acres of poor farmland flooded to make a series of breathtaking waterscapes. With its tales of mass trespass and pioneering access agreements, this is the heartland of the English rambling tradition. But the walking here can be harder than it is in the limestone dales to the south. The weather can quickly take a dramatic turn for the worse, even on a sunny day, and navigation can become more problematic as the moors are engulfed in impenetrable cloud. The highest points of Kinder and Bleaklow surpass 2,000ft (610m) and heavy snowfall is not uncommon in the winter months.

White Peak

Gentler walking can be found in the southern half of the district. The White Peak takes its name from the limestone which dominates the scenery. Here you will find tiny valleys carved into the plateau, Lathkill Dale, Monsal Dale, Mill Dale and Wolfscote Dale. Perhaps the most famous is Dovedale, chaperoning the River Dove through a landscape of bizarre rock pinnacles and caves steeped in mythology. The River Manifold too, cuts a dramatic gorge, flanked by limestone

Right: Damflask Reservoir, Bradfield Dale, near Sheffield (Walk 7)

crags and mysterious chasms. You'll find many pretty villages here as well – Tissington, Hartington, Youlgreave and Ashford in the Water – fine places to take afternoon tea or relax in a friendly pub. The Derwent Valley momentarily opens out, south of Baslow, making space for the parklands surrounding Chatsworth House. Here the Duke of Devonshire's palatial home sits in a splendid green vale, with gritstone edges to the east and limestone dales to the west.

Gritstone Fringe

Fingers of gritstone surround the White Peak, giving Cheshire and Staffordshire a valuable moorland fringe and lingering in the east so that even Chesterfield can catch a piece in the delightful Linacre Valley. From Crich Stand the defiant heights look out over much plainer territory. You can follow a gritstone trail along the serene edges overlooking Bollington and Macclesfield, or linger around the shores of Tittesworth Reservoir, or the rocky towers of the Roaches. On these quiet heights it seems barely credible that a third of England's population lives less than one hour's drive away.

Industrial Relics

Industry has always tried to tame this landscape, but somehow the remains of the mills, lead mines, quarries and railways have blended in to add to its romance. Certainly the easy access afforded to walkers by trails on former railway trackbeds has added greatly to the Peak District's charm. Where steam trains once wound their tedious course through Monsal Dale or across the limestone plateau, so the modern walker can now stride in confidence on the Tissington, High Peak and Monsal trails. Before the railways it was the 'Jaggers' with their trains of packhorses who crossed these hills. Now you can follow their routes over high moors and through lonely dale heads, perhaps with a hint of gratitude for their eye for an easy gradient and a well-placed bridge. They carried salt and coal through this beautiful landscape long before anyone considered it to be one worth preserving.

Beyond the National Park

Beyond the national park, the Midland plain reaches up to capture the towns and villages of South Derbyshire. Here you will find a very different walking experience, in the parkland of great houses such as Melbourne, Markeaton, Osmaston, Shirley and Calke Abbey. But don't overlook it. The character of the landscape may be very different from that of the Peak District proper, but for many its warm brick-built buildings will provide a welcome contrast to the ubiquitous stone of its northern neighbours.

Snapshot

These 50 walks represent a snapshot of the opportunities available to those prepared to muddy their feet and stray off the beaten path. From high points to low, light to dark you'll find the Peak District has a lot more to offer the walker than tea shops and show caves, and I hope that the walks in this book inspire you to return to the many delights of the Peak District again and again.

Using this book

INFORMATION PANELS

An information panel for each walk shows its relative difficulty (see Walk 5), the distance and total amount of ascent. An indication of the gradients you will encounter is shown by the rating ▲ ▲ ▲ (no steep slopes) to ▲ ▲ ▲ (several very steep slopes).

MAPS

There are 50 maps, covering the walks. Some walks have a suggested option in the same area. The information panel for these walks will tell you how much extra walking is involved. On short-cut suggestions the panel will tell you the total distance if you set out from the start of the main walk. Where an option returns to the same point on the main walk, just the distance of the loop is given. Where an option leaves the main walk at one point and returns to it at another, then the distance shown is for the whole walk. The minimum time suggested is for reasonably fit walkers and doesn't allow for stops. Each walk has a suggested Ordnance Survey map.

START POINTS

The start of each walk is given as a six-figure grid reference prefixed by two letters indicating which 100-km square of the National Grid it refers to. You'll find more information on grid references on most Ordnance Survey maps.

DOGS

We have tried to give dog owners useful advice about how dog friendly each walk is. Please respect other countryside users. Keep your dog under control, especially around livestock, and obey local bylaws and other dog control notices.

CAR PARKING

Many of the car parks suggested are public, but occasionally you may find you have to park on the roadside or in a lay-by. Please be considerate when you leave your car, ensuring that access roads or gates are not blocked and that other vehicles can pass safely.

Right: Footpath up to Mam Tor, Peak District National Park (Walk 11)

Along the Colne Valley

The rural face of the valley between Slaithwaite and Marsden.

> **DISTANCE** 6 miles (9.7km)   **MINIMUM TIME** 3hrs 30min
>
> **ASCENT/GRADIENT** 550ft (170m) ▲▲▲   **LEVEL OF DIFFICULTY** +++
>
> **PATHS** Field paths, good tracks and canal tow path, many stiles
>
> **LANDSCAPE** Typical South Pennine country, canalside
>
> **SUGGESTED MAP** OS Explorer OL21 South Pennines
>
> **START / FINISH** Grid reference: SE 079140
>
> **DOG FRIENDLINESS** Tow path is especially good for dogs
>
> **PARKING** Plenty of street parking in Slaithwaite
>
> **PUBLIC TOILETS** Slaithwaite and Marsden

Transport across the Pennine watershed has always presented problems. The Leeds and Liverpool Canal, built during the 1770s, took a convoluted route across the Pennines, through the Aire Gap at Skipton. Then came the Rochdale Canal. However, its more direct route came at a high price: mile for mile, this canal has more locks than any other inland waterway in the country. With the increase in trade between Yorkshire and Lancashire, a third route across the Pennines was soon needed. The Huddersfield Narrow Canal links Huddersfield with Ashton-under-Lyne in Greater Manchester. Though only 20 miles (32.2km) long, it includes the Standedge Tunnel (see Walk 2). Begun in 1798, and dug with pick, shovel and dynamite, the canal was opened to traffic in 1811.

Beads on a String

The Colne Valley, to the west of Huddersfield, is representative of industrial West Yorkshire. Towns with evocative names – Milnsbridge, Linthwaite, Slaithwaite and Marsden – are threaded along the River Colne like beads on a string. In the 18th century this was a landscape of scattered farms and hand-loom weavers, mostly situated on the higher ground. As with Calderdale, a few miles to the north, the deep-cut valley of the Colne was transformed by the Industrial Revolution. Once the textile processes began to be mechanised, mills were built in the valley bottom by the new breed of industrial entrepreneurs. They specialised in the production of fine worsted cloth.

The River Colne provided the power for the first mills, and the canal subsequently improved the transport links. The mills grew larger as water power gave way to steam, towering over the rows of terraced houses built in their shadows. Throughout this walk you can see the mill chimneys and the sawtooth roof-lines of the weaving sheds, though some mills are ruinous and others are now given over to other trades.

Slaithwaite (often pronounced 'Slowitt') is typical of the textile towns in the Colne Valley: unpretentious, a little bit scruffy. It looks to be an unlikely spa town. But that's what it became, albeit briefly, when its mineral springs were compared favourably with those of Harrogate. The town is now undergoing a facelift and its canal is being restored.

SLAITHWAITE

Golcar

Colne Valley Museum

↑ Huddersfield

Linthwaite

297 ▲

A62

Slaithwaite

Black Moor

← N →

1 BRITANNIA ROAD

VARLEY ROAD

B6109

Meltham →

B6107

HOLLINS LANE

2

328 ▲

Deer Hill Reservoir

Huddersfield Narrow Canal

A62

B6107

326 ▲

3

354 ▲

Holme Moor

Netherwood Heys

Hard Hill

Slaithwaite Moor

0 ½ mile

0 1 km

5

Marsden

STATION RD

FALL LA

Bank Bottom Mills

4

Butterley Res

WALK 1 DIRECTIONS

1 Walk along Britannia Road and at the end go right, up to the A62. Cross over and walk up Varley Road. Beyond the last house go right, through a stile next to a gate. Join a track across a field to a stile on the right-hand end of the wall ahead. Follow a wall to your right, across a stile, to a minor road. Go right and follow the road left to a crossroads. Go straight ahead on a track; after just 20yds (18m) bear left on a track between houses. Squeeze past a gate on to a field path. Follow a wall on your right; towards its end go through a gap and take the steps in the same direction. Follow the obvious route downhill to the road.

2 Go right, along the road, for 20yds (18m) and then turn left on to a track (signed 'Hollins Lane'). Continue as the track becomes rougher; when it peters out, keep left of a cottage and go through a gate. Follow a field-edge path ahead, through a pair of gates either side of a beck. Pass a ruined house to descend on a walled path. When it bears sharp right keep ahead to go through a gate on to a field path. Follow a wall on your right; where it ends keep ahead, slightly uphill across two fields, and meet a walled track. Go left here, towards a farm. Go right, after 50yds (46m), through a stile, on to a path downhill. It soon bears right; take a stile to the left to follow a field-edge path.

Cross another field, go through a kissing gate and turn to walk uphill to reach a path that leads up to the B6107.

3 Go right, along the road, for just 75yds (68m), and take a track to your left. Keep left of a house, via a gate. About 150yds (138m) past the house bear right at a fork, taking the less obvious track. You soon follow a wall, beginning a slow descent. Across a beck, the track forks again; keep left, uphill, to skirt the shoulder of much-quarried Hard Hill. The track takes you steeply downhill, then up to a kissing gate, then down again to cross a beck on a stone retaining wall. After another little climb, you have level walking with Butterley Reservoir ahead of you. Bear left, steeply uphill, at a tiny stone building, cross two stiles and meet a tarmac track. Follow it right, downhill, to meet a road.

4 Go right, down the road, passing terraced houses dwarfed by Bank Bottom Mills. Keep straight ahead at the roundabout, down Fall Lane, soon bearing left to dip beneath the main road and fork left into Marsden. Take Station Road, at the far end of a green, up to meet the Huddersfield Narrow Canal.

5 Take a path on the right that soon joins the canal tow path. Follow the canal tow path for about 3 miles (4.8km), passing beneath a road, past numerous locks and a couple of road bridges back into Slaithwaite.

WHERE TO EAT AND DRINK

You have a wide choice of pubs and cafés on this walk, in both Slaithwaite and Marsden. The Railway, close to the rail station and canal, in Marsden, comes at the half-way point of the walk.

EXTENDING THE WALK

To learn more about the area, you can continue walking alongside the canal into the mill village of Golcar, where you will find the interesting Colne Valley Museum in a weaver's cottage on the hill.

Standedge from Marsden

A classic moorland ramble on the ancient Rapes Highway.

DISTANCE 6.5 miles (10.4km)   MINIMUM TIME 3hrs 30min

ASCENT/GRADIENT 900ft (375m) ▲▲▲   LEVEL OF DIFFICULTY ✚✚✚

PATHS Old tracks and byways, canal tow path, a few stiles

LANDSCAPE Heather moorland

SUGGESTED MAP OS Explorer OL21 South Pennines

START / FINISH Grid reference: SE 048117

DOG FRIENDLINESS Keep under control where sheep graze on open moorland

PARKING Free street parking in Marsden

PUBLIC TOILETS Marsden, at start of walk

Trans-Pennine travel has, until quite recently, been a hazardous business. Over the centuries many routes have been driven across the hills to link the industrial centres of West Yorkshire and Lancashire. Some paths were consolidated into paved causeways for packhorse traffic, before being upgraded to take vehicles. This track, linking the Colne Valley to Rochdale and Milnrow in Lancashire, was known as the Rapes Highway.

The Standedge Tunnel

This was tough terrain for building a canal. When the Huddersfield Narrow Canal was cut, to provide a link between Huddersfield and Ashton-under-Lyne, there was one major obstacle for the canal builders to overcome – the gritstone bulk of Standedge. There was no way round; the canal had to go through. The Standedge Tunnel, extending 3 miles (4.8km) from Marsden to Diggle, was a monumental feat of engineering. Costly in every sense, it took 16 years to build and many navvies lost their lives. The result was the longest, highest and deepest canal tunnel in the country.

In an attempt to keep those costs down, the tunnel was cut as narrow as possible, which left no room for a tow path. Towing horses had to be led over the hills to the far end of the tunnel, near Diggle in Lancashire. The bargees had to negotiate Standedge Tunnel using their own muscle power alone. This method, known as 'legging', required them to lie on their backs and push with their feet against the sides and roof of the tunnel. This operation would typically take a back-breaking 4 hours; it would have been a great relief to see the proverbial light at the end of the tunnel. Closed to canal traffic for many years, the tunnel was reopened in 2001. It is now a major tourist attraction and includes boat trips and a visitor centre.

In 1812 Marsden became the focus for the 'Luddite' rebellion against mechanisation in the textile industry. A secret group of croppers and weavers banded together to break up the new machinery which was appearing in local mills and which had been developed by local industrialists. Eventually the army was despatched to restore order. Sixty men were put on trial in York for their part in the troubles; 17 of them were subsequently hanged.

WALK

2

Castleshaw
Moor

*Castleshaw
Upper
Reservoir*

447 ▲

PENNINE WAY

A640

4

448 ▲
March Hill

Oldgate
Moss

*March
Haigh
Reservoir*

378 ▲

Millstone
Edge

5 ▲ 448

C l o s e
M o s s

Haigh Clough

Oakner Clough

3

*Brun
Clough
Reservoir*

P

6

Oldham

Redbrook Clough

Closegate
or Eastergate
Bridge

Hey
Green
Hotel

WATERS ROAD

A62

*Redbrook
Reservoir*

437 ▲
Pule Hill

Tunnel End
Inn

*Huddersfield
Narrow Canal*

2

PENNINE WAY

▲ 412
Bobus

7

Hades
Farm

STATION
ROAD

OLD MOUNT ROAD

1

*Butterley
Reservoir*

Marsden

Huddersfield

0   ½ mile
0   1 km

WALK 2 DIRECTIONS

1 From the centre of Marsden, take Station Road, uphill. Between the Railway pub, and the station itself, go left along the tow path of the Huddersfield Narrow Canal. At Tunnel End, where both canal and train lines disappear into a tunnel through the hillside, go across over the canal on a footbridge, and walk up the tarmac drive past the visitor exhibition to the Tunnel End Inn.

2 Turn left on to Waters Road. Go through a gate on the left for a path parallel to the road. After rejoining, keep straight ahead at the entrance to the Hey Green Hotel. 100yds (91m) further on, bear left, just before a cottage, on to a footpath. The path takes you across Closegate Bridge, known locally as Eastergate Bridge, where two becks meet.

WHERE TO EAT AND DRINK

The café by the entrance to the Standedge Tunnel serves light refreshments, or for more standard pub fare try the Tunnel End Inn, just up the hill where walkers are very welcome and the food is served daily.

3 Keep right, following the right-hand beck for about 100yds (91m), when the path bears left, up a steep side-valley. The path levels off at the top and then bears slightly right, towards the rounded prominence of March Hill. Your route across moorland is soon marked by a series of waymarker stones. After a few ups and downs, the path rises steeply uphill, before descending towards the A640.

4 Just before you reach the road, take a wooden bridge over a little beck and follow a Pennine Way sign on a track that bears acute left. Take this well-maintained gravel track uphill. After a few minutes you follow the contours of Millstone Edge, a rocky ridge that offers panoramic views into East Lancashire.

5 After enjoying views at the trig point, your route is downhill. Take a succession of stiles in walls and fences before turning left on an unmade track that leads down to the A62, where a car park overlooks Brun Clough Reservoir.

6 Cross the road and take steps up to the left of the car park, signed 'Pennine Way', to access a good track, soon revealing views to the left of Redbrook Reservoir and Pule Hill beyond. At a marker stone the Pennine Way bears right. But your route, having made a small detour to cross a tiny beck, is to continue along the track. It gradually sweeps left, around the slopes of Pule Hill, to reach a road.

7 Turn right, along the road, but then immediately left, up Old Mount Road. After 100yds (91m), bear left again, up a stony track signed to Hades Farm. After 0.5 mile (800m), take a path to the right, that accompanies a wall, to rejoin Old Mount Road. Follow the road downhill to arrive back in Marsden again.

WHAT TO LOOK OUT FOR

In spring and early summer, listen out for the cuckoo. If an old story is to be believed, the people of Marsden realised that when the cuckoo arrived, so did the sunshine. They tried to keep spring forever, by building a tower around the cuckoo. As the last stones were about to be laid, however, the cuckoo flew away. The folk of Marsden celebrate Cuckoo Day in April each year.

A Taste of the Last of the Summer Wine

Follow in the footsteps of the immortal Compo, Foggy and Clegg.

3

DISTANCE 4.5 miles (7.2km)	**MINIMUM TIME** 2hrs 30min

ASCENT/GRADIENT 558ft (170m) ▲▲▲ **LEVEL OF DIFFICULTY** ✦✦✦

PATHS Good paths and tracks, plenty of stiles

LANDSCAPE Upland pasture

SUGGESTED MAP OS Explorer 288 Bradford & Huddersfield

START / FINISH Grid reference: SE 143084

DOG FRIENDLINESS On lead in fields with livestock, off on lanes

PARKING Centre of Holmfirth gets very crowded, so park in Crown Bottom car park (pay-and-display) on Huddersfield Road

PUBLIC TOILETS Holmfirth

Holmfirth and the Holme Valley have been popularised as 'Summer Wine Country'. The whimsical TV series, starring the trio of incorrigible old buffers Compo, Foggy and Clegg, has now been running for a quarter of a century. These larger-than-life characters, going back to their second childhoods, have proved to be an irresistible formula in the hands of writer Roy Clarke.

Last of the Summer Wine was first seen in January 1973, as a one-off Comedy Playhouse episode. The response was so good that a six-part series was commissioned. The rest is history, with *Summer Wine* becoming the UK's longest running comedy programme.

The cast have become familiar faces around Holmfirth. So much so that when Londoner Bill Owen (lovable rogue 'Compo') died in 1999 at the age of 85, he was laid to rest overlooking the little town he had grown to call home. Bill Owen's real-life son Tom joined the cast to play Compo's long lost son, and together with plenty of newcomers, the series seems to have plenty of life in it yet.

Visitors come to Holmfirth in their droves, in search of film locations such as Sid's Café and Nora Batty's house. But Holmfirth takes its TV fame in its stride, for this isn't the first time that the town has starred in front of the cameras. In fact, Holmfirth very nearly became another Hollywood. Bamforths – better known for its naughty seaside postcards – began to make short films here in the early years of the last century. They were exported around the world to popular demand. Local people were drafted in as extras in Bamforths' overwrought dramas. Film production came to an end at the outbreak of the First World War and, sadly, was never resumed.

Holmfirth

Holmfirth town, much more than just a film set, is the real star – along with the fine South Pennine scenery which surrounds it. By the time you have completed half of this walk, you are a mile (1.6km) from the Peak National Park.

The town grew rapidly with the textile trades, creating a tight-knit community in the valley bottom: a maze of ginnels, alleyways and narrow lanes. The River Holme, which runs through its middle, has flooded on many occasions. But the most devastating flood occurred back in 1852 when, after heavy rain, Bilberry Reservoir burst its banks. The resulting torrent of water destroyed the centre of Holmfirth and claimed 81 lives. The tragedy was reported at length on the front page of the *London Illustrated News*, complete with an artist's impression of the devastation. A public subscription fund was started to help the flood survivors to rebuild the town. These traumatic events are marked by a monument situated near the bus station.

WALK 3 DIRECTIONS

1 From Crown Bottom car park, walk to the right along Huddersfield Road for just 100yds (91m) before bearing left opposite the fire station, up Wood Lane. The road soon narrows to a steep track. Keep left of a house and through a gate, to continue on a walled path. At the top of the hill, by a bench, follow the track to the right. Follow this track, soon enclosed, as it wheels left, down into a valley. Soon after you approach woodland, you have a choice of tracks: keep left on the walled path, uphill. Join a more substantial farm track and approaching a building on the top of the track, take the second stile on the left, across a field

WHERE TO EAT AND DRINK

With so many visitors, Holmfirth is well supplied with pubs and tea shops, where you can stop for refreshments. Sid's Café and The Wrinkled Stocking Café (next to Nora Batty's steps) will already be familiar to fans of *Last of the Summer Wine*.

path to emerge by the houses of Upperthong. Turn left and follow the road as it bends through the top of the village.

2 Continue along the road, which wheels round to the right. Walk downhill, with great views opening up of the Holme Valley. After 150yds (138m) on the road, take a cinder track on the right. Walk down past Newlands Farm to meet a road. Cross over and take the lane ahead, steeply down into a little valley and up the other side. When this minor road forks at the top, go right, uphill. Immediately after the first house, go left, on a gravel track. Follow this track to Lower Hogley Farm where you keep right, past a knot of houses, to a gate and on to a field path, with a wall to your left. Go through three more fields, aiming for the mast on the horizon, and descend to the road.

3 Go right for just 50yds (46m) to bear left around an old schoolhouse on a grassy path. Follow the walled footpath downhill, through a gate; as the footpath opens out into a grassy area, bear left on a grassy track down into the valley. Follow a high stone wall on your right-hand side, over a stile, on to an enclosed path. On approaching houses, take a stile and join a metalled track at a fork. Bear right here, then immediately left, on a narrow footpath between houses. Follow

a field path through a gate; pass houses and a mill down to meet the main A6024 road.

4 Cross the road then, by a row of diminutive cottages, take Old Road to the left. Keep straight ahead when you reach a junction, down Water Street. Beyond a mill, cross the River Holme on a metal footbridge and follow a riverside path. Soon the footpath veers right through pasture; when the path forks, keep to the right, uphill, to enter woodland.

WHILE YOU'RE THERE

If you drive through Holmfirth on the A6024, you pass Holmbridge, then Holme, before the Holme Valley comes to a dramatic end, surrounded by a huge sweep of rugged moorland and splendid views. As you climb steeply to the height of Holme Moss, topped with a television mast, you enter the Peak National Park.

Continue in the same direction, uphill, swinging left to pass below an old quarry in the woods, then forking right (uphill) to emerge at a field. Cross two fields and join a track by a house. Pass some more cottages to meet a road.

5 Go left, along the road. Enjoy fine views down into the Holme Valley, as you make the long descent back to Holmfirth.

WHAT TO LOOK OUT FOR

Holmfirth seems to have grown without much help from town planners. It is an intriguing maze of ginnels, stone steps and small cobbled alleyways, rising up between gritstone houses. After a few minutes' climb you will be rewarded with a view over the roofscape of the town.

Quenching the Thirst at Dovestones

A circular walk around the moorland reservoirs near Uppermill.

DISTANCE 7 miles (11.3km)   MINIMUM TIME 4hrs
ASCENT/GRADIENT 1,445ft (440m)▲▲▲ LEVEL OF DIFFICULTY ✦✦✦
PATHS Generally hard and rocky, some boggy patches on moorland top
LANDSCAPE Steep hillsides with rocky outcrops and open moorland
SUGGESTED MAP OS Explorer OL1 Dark Peak
START / FINISH Grid reference: SE 013036
DOG FRIENDLINESS Mostly open sheep country subject to access agreements, dogs should be kept on lead or close control at all times
PARKING Car park below Dovestone Reservoir dam (daily charge)
PUBLIC TOILETS By car park

Around 130 years ago, as the demands of Manchester's industrial population grew, the need to supply the city with safe and sufficient drinking water became paramount. Inevitably the planners turned their attentions towards the Pennines, that formidable upland barrier that soaks up so much of northern England's rain. Before long a series of reservoirs sprung up across the hills that separated urban Lancashire and Yorkshire and, just as the counties' rivers and streams had previously been harnessed for the mills, now the moorlands were drained and the tiny Pennine valleys dammed to create artificial lakes. The first of the four reservoirs collectively known as Dovestones was Yeoman Hey, constructed in 1880, and followed by Greenfield in 1902. When Chew Reservoir was built, ten years later, it was the highest in Britain at around 1,600ft (488m). Dovestone Reservoir is the largest of the group and was completed in 1967.

Four Reservoirs

Today the four vital reservoirs supply drinking water to Oldham and communities in the Tame Valley. They are owned and run by United Utilities, who provide water to nearly 3 million people in North West England. In total the water company owns around 140,000 acres (56,700ha) of water-gathering land and actual reservoirs throughout the Peak District, Lake District and West Pennines. Here at Dovestones water collects in Chew Reservoir, high and remote on the top of the bleak moorland, before travelling via an underground pipe almost a mile (1.6km) long to emerge at an aqueduct at Ashway Gap, below Dean Rocks. Water is then held in the two main reservoirs in the valley bottom, Dovestone and Yeoman Hey, before being piped further down the valley for treatment at a large plant at Buckton Castle in Mossley. It's also used by a paper mill located below Dovestone Reservoir dam.

Recreation

United Utilities actively encourages certain types of recreation around its reservoirs. Swimming is forbidden, because of the deep water and outlet pipes that can cause dangerous undercurrents, but sailing and windsurfing take place

WALK 4

on Dovestone Reservoir, with regular regattas. On the adjoining hillside there are two terrific orienteering routes – look out for the small posts with helpful coloured markings and numbers.

The popular 2.5-mile (4km) track around the shore of Dovestone Reservoir has been made suitable for wheelchair users, while the numerous paths and bridleways that explore the surrounding moors also include the Oldham Way. The course of this superb circular, 40-mile (64.3km) walking route around the borough of Oldham can be seen as you set off from Dovestone Reservoir. It runs high and straight across the hillside to the south, on the route of a former steam tramway that was built 90 years ago to aid the construction of Chew Reservoir.

WALK 4 DIRECTIONS

❶ From the car park walk up to the top of the Dovestone Reservoir dam and turn right, along the road past the sailing club. Where the plantation ends go over a bridge and straight on to

follow a private, vehicular track as it makes its way steadily up to the very top of the Chew Valley.

❷ When you reach Chew Reservoir turn left and walk along by the dam wall until just before it kinks right. With your back to the

DOVESTONE RESERVOIR

reservoir (and near a sign warning of the dangers of deep water) drop down to the moorland and follow the very wide, straight track opposite that heads back towards the edge of the hillside. It first bears left, then swings back to the right, and soon becomes a thin path that weaves its way between the loose rocks around Dish Stone Brow.

3 With Dovestone Reservoir coming into view far below, continue along the high rim of the hillside past a series of rocky outcrops. If you occasionally lose sight of the path don't worry, just keep to the wide strip between the steep drop on your left and the banks of peaty bog on your right.

4 Nearing Great Dove Stone Rocks continue to follow the rocky edge as it swings back to the right. Beyond Dean Rocks is a clear path that winds its way around the head of a narrow valley known as Dove Stone Clough.

5 Cross over the stream as it flows over a rocky shelf and, as you continue across the slope on the far side, the narrow path slowly begins to drop down the grassy hillside. Fork left and ignore a higher path towards a

prominent stone memorial cross ahead. Soon the path curves steeply down to the left and there are numerous criss-crossing tracks through the long grass and bracken. If you are in any doubt then just aim for the unmistakable aqueduct below you, at the foot of Dove Stone Clough, and cross it by using the high footbridge.

6 Walk along the path below the rock face and the fence on your left and across an area of slumped hillside littered with rock debris. Eventually the path joins a wide, grassy strip that gently leads down between fenced-off plantations of young conifers. Go through the gate and drop down through the open field to reach the popular reservoir-side track. Turn left and then follow this track all the way back to the car park.

Overleaf: View across Longdendale Vale (Walk 5)

Manchester's Bit of Derbyshire

In Longdendale, the wild Pennines meet the bustling metropolis.

DISTANCE 7.5 miles (12.1km) **MINIMUM TIME** 4hrs

ASCENT/GRADIENT 1,180ft (360m) ▲▲▲ **LEVEL OF DIFFICULTY** +++

PATHS Good paths and tracks, a few stiles

LANDSCAPE Heather moorland, and rolling farm pastures

SUGGESTED MAP OS Explorer OL1 Dark Peak

START / FINISH Grid reference: SK 073994

DOG FRIENDLINESS Walk is on farmland and access agreement land, dogs should be kept on lead

PARKING Crowden pay car park

PUBLIC TOILETS At car park and Torside car park

Longdendale, the valley of the River Etherow, threads deep into the Pennines between the craggy cliffs of Bleaklow and the sullen slopes of Black Hill. In bygone centuries this must have been an inhospitable but dramatic wilderness of heath and bog.

Meanwhile in nearby Manchester, the Industrial Revolution had caused a dramatic increase in the population from around 10,000 to over 230,000. This meant that Manchester needed more water, and its engineers turned to Longdendale. Between 1848 and 1877 a string of five reservoirs were built to the designs of John Frederic La Trobe Bateman. Later came the railway, linking Manchester with Sheffield, then came electricity. So this remote narrow valley was filled with the contraptions of the modern world. Manchester's people came here in their thousands, using the railway and taking to the hills.

Pennine Wayfarers

Crowden, where the walk starts, is one of the few settlements in the valley. Around the youth hostel you'll often see weary walkers, weighed down with heavy backpacks. More often than not they will have just completed the first day of the Pennine Way over Kinder Scout and Bleaklow. In the little book they're clutching Alfred Wainwright has told them how unsightly Longdendale is, and how they will continue towards the horrors of Black Hill's bogs.

But this walk shows you the very best of Longdendale. The railway has gone now, dismantled in 1981 with the decline of the coal industry. After strolling down to the Torside Reservoir you follow its trackbed, now part of the Longdendale Trail. Soon you've left the valley behind and you're climbing through the shade of woods, where oak, birch, larch and pine are mixed with open patches of heather and bilberry. Longdendale looks pretty good now. Bleaklow's ruffled peat-hagged top is fronted by a bold line of cliffs, which overlook the valley's blue lakes and emerald fields. Several streams plummet down shady ravines, while Torside Clough, a huge gash in the side of the fell, dwarfs the little farm at its foot.

Now you're on the moors with squat cliffs of Millstone Rocks lying across cotton grass moors. At Lad's Leap, the Hollins Clough stream tumbles over a slabbed rocky bed into Coombes Clough. I don't know who the lad was that could leap across this gap, but he must have had long legs, or a good imagination. Mere mortals descend to ford the stream before continuing above Highstone Rocks to the rim of the Crowden valley where you can look deep into the inner recesses of Black Hill. Below, just a short descent away, your car awaits.

WALK 5 DIRECTIONS

❶ Leave the car park and cross the A628. Take the permissive footpath east before crossing a footbridge over the Etherow beneath the Woodhead dam. Passing through a small wood, the path meets a road. Cross it to join the Longdendale and Trans Pennine Trails.

❷ Turn right along the trackbed, following the two trails westwards above the south shore of Torside Reservoir. Leave the track where it crosses the road, then follow the lane opposite, crossing the dam to the north shore. At the apex of a right-hand bend leave the lane for another permissive footpath, this time heading west above Rhodeswood Reservoir.

3 After going through the left of two gates, follow the path through some scrub woodland to reach the Rhodeswood dam, where a tarmac lane takes you back to the main road.

4 Turn left along the road for a few paces, then cross it to climb on a track right of the intake wall. Turn right to follow an old quarry track that zig-zags up heather and grass slopes before delving into the woods of Didsbury Intake. The track passes between the cliffs and the bouldery landslip area of Tintwistle Knarr Quarry.

5 After leaving the woods behind you reach the brim of the moor by Rawkins Brook. Go over the stile in the fence and trace a peaty path known as Black Gutter. This heads roughly north-east across heathland towards the gritstone 'edge' of Millstone Rocks.

6 Follow the edge to Lad's Leap, where you descend to ford the Hollins Clough stream before

climbing back on to the moors. A dilapidated wall comes in from the right, and the path descends with it into the Crowden valley.

7 Half-way down the slope it meets the Pennine Way route, where you turn right, descending towards Torside Reservoir.

8 Turn left along a prominent unsurfaced lane that descends parallel to the northern shore of the reservoir and then to the bottom of the Crowden valley. Walk across the bridge over Crowden Brook, then follow the walled lane as it curves right to reach a crossroads. Turn right, passing the campsite and toilet block, to return to the car park.

Avoiding the Black Stuff

There is more to the peatlands of Bleaklow than mile upon mile of bog.

> **DISTANCE** 7 miles (11.3km)   **MINIMUM TIME** 4hrs
> **ASCENT/GRADIENT** 1,500ft (460m) ▲▲   **LEVEL OF DIFFICULTY** +++
> **PATHS** Unsurfaced tracks and moorland paths, a few stiles
> **LANDSCAPE** High peat moor
> **SUGGESTED MAP** OS Explorer OL1 Dark Peak
> **START / FINISH** Grid reference: SK 043947
> **DOG FRIENDLINESS** Access agreement land, dogs should be kept on lead
> **PARKING** Manor Park car park, off Glossop High Street East (A57)
> **PUBLIC TOILETS** At car park

Bleaklow's not so much a hill, more a vast expanse of bare black peat, where even the toughest moor grasses can't take root. Wainwright once wrote that nobody loved the place, and those who got on it were glad to get off. But there's another side to Bleaklow. There are corners where bilberries grow thick round fascinating rock sculptures; where heather, bracken and grass weave a colourful quilt draped beneath wide skies. Places like Grinah Stones, Yellowslacks and Shepherd's Meeting Stones are all remote, but they're dramatic places, far superior to anything seen on the popular routes. Bleaklow's true top lies in the midst of the mires, but only a few feet lower is Higher Shelf Stones, a bold summit with a distinctive mountain shape – and some good crags. Climb Higher Shelf Stones from Old Glossop, and you'll see the best of Bleaklow.

Old Glossop
Time has been kind to Old Glossop. Planners and industrialists of the 19th and 20th centuries built their shops and factories further west, leaving the old quarter untouched. Here 17th-century cottages of darkened gritstone line cobbled streets, overlooked by the spired All Saints Church. Shepley Street takes you into the hills, and it's not long before you're climbing the heathery spur of Lightside and looking across the rocky ravine of Yellowslacks. A fine path develops on the cliff-edge before entering the confines of Dowstone Clough, which clambers towards Higher Shelf Stones. Eventually the clough shallows and the stream becomes a trickle in the peat, leaving you to find your own way. Sandy channels, known as groughs, lead you southwards.

Higher Shelf Stones
Suddenly, the peat ends and the trig point appears. From the summit rocks you look down on the deep twisting clough of Shelf Brook and out across the plains of Manchester to the shadowy hills of North Wales. It's time to leave the high moors. There's a faint path across a grassy spur descending into Shelf Brook's clough, where you join the Doctor's Gate track. This gets its name from John Talbot, the Vicar of Glossop 1450–94, who often used the road to visit his father in Sheffield.

GLOSSOP

WALK 6

His trips were worthy of note because he was in fact the illegitimate son of the very powerful, Earl of Shrewsbury. Much earlier, the old highway was used by Roman troops marching between their forts at Navio (Brough, near Hope) and Melandra (Glossop). We follow their footsteps as the paved track twists through the clough, by the rounded Shire Hill and back to Old Glossop.

WALK 6 DIRECTIONS

1 From the car park, walk through Manor Park and then turn left along Manor Park Road into Old Glossop. Turn right along Shepley Street, passing the factory to the bus turning circle. Here a farm track continues eastwards, with the partially wooded dome of Shire Hill on the right and the pine and oak-clad slopes of Edge Plantation on the left.

2 Leave the track at a ladder stile. Cross the stile on to a path, confined at first by a fence and dry-stone wall, that climbs north-east on a pastured spur overlooking the curiously named but pleasant craggy valley of Shittern Clough. In the upper reaches and beyond a second ladder stile, the now well-defined path continues the climb through bilberry bushes and then over the heather of Upper Lightside.

❸ A narrow path switches to the spur's southern brow high above Yellowslacks Brook. A dilapidated wire fence comes in from the right and the path goes along the right-hand side of it before joining the cliff edges of Yellowslacks and Dog Rock. The crags close in to form the rugged channel of Dowstone Clough. The path, now intermittent, stays close to the stream and keeps away from the peat hags.

❹ As the clough shallows and the stream divides among a bed of rushes (grid ref 089954), aim for Higher Shelf Stones by crossing the main stream and following its southbound tributary – just follow the bootprints along its sandy bed, which snakes through a complex of peat hags in a southbound direction. Near the summit of Higher Shelf Stones the channel shallows and widens then, suddenly, the trig point rises from a grassy plinth ahead.

❺ From Higher Shelf Stones, trace the brow of Shelf Moor towards Lower Shelf Stones then on to James's Thorn, on a narrow path, but circumvent the naked peat that proliferates on the left. A prominent grassy channel

descends just north of west and forms a reliable and reasonably dry course down over Shelf Moor to a boulder strewn edge above Ferny Hole.

❻ From here down to the Doctor's Gate path, soon visible far below, follow a faint but discernible path that weaves its way down the rough hillside east of Shelf Benches. Towards the bottom, it merges with a wider, grassy track and joins Doctor's Gate by a stone barn. Continue down the valley.

❼ Doctor's Gate meanders through the moorland clough of Shelf Brook before passing Mossy Lea Farm. Continue straight on to join the outward route at the foot of Lightside and brings you back to Old Glossop.

Bradfield and the Dale Dike Dam Disaster

A quiet waterside walk around the site of a horrific 19th-century industrial tragedy.

DISTANCE *5.5 miles (8.8km)* **MINIMUM TIME** *3hrs 30min*

ASCENT/GRADIENT *394ft (120m)* ▲▲▲ **LEVEL OF DIFFICULTY** ✦✦✦

PATHS *Minor roads, bridleways, forest paths*

LANDSCAPE *Woodland, reservoir and meadows*

SUGGESTED MAP *OS Explorer OL1 Dark Peak*

START / FINISH *Grid reference: SK 262920*

DOG FRIENDLINESS *Keep on lead near livestock*

PARKING *Car park by Low Bradfield cricket ground*

PUBLIC TOILETS *Low Bradfield, near post office*

Just before midnight on Friday 11 March 1864, when the Dale Dike Dam tragically collapsed, 650 million gallons (2,955 million litres) of water surged along the Loxley Valley towards Sheffield, leaving a trail of death and destruction. When the floods finally subsided 244 people had been killed and hundreds of properties destroyed.

The Bradfield Scheme

During the Industrial Revolution Sheffield expanded rapidly, as country people sought employment in the city's steel and cutlery works. This put considerable pressure on the water supply. The 'Bradfield Scheme' was Sheffield Waterworks Company's ambitious proposal to build massive reservoirs in the hills around the village of Bradfield, about 8 miles (12.9km) from the city. Work commenced on the first of these, the Dale Dike Dam on 1 January 1859. It was a giant by the standards of the time with a capacity of over 700 million gallons (3,182 million litres) of water, but some 200 million gallons (910 million litres) less than the present reservoir.

The Disaster of 1864

Construction of the dam continued until late February 1864, by which time the reservoir was almost full. Friday 11 March was a stormy day and as one of the dam workers crossed the earthen embankment on his way home, he noticed a crack, about a finger's width, running along it. John Gunson the chief engineer turned out with one of the contractors to inspect the dam. They had to make the 8 miles (12.9km) from Sheffield in a horse-drawn gig, in deteriorating weather conditions, so it was 10pm before they got there. After an initial inspection, Gunson concluded that it was probably nothing to worry about. However as a precaution he decided to lower the water level. He re-inspected the crack at 11.30pm, noting that it had not visibly deteriorated. However, then the engineer saw to his horror that water was running over the top of the embankment into the crack. He was making his way to the bottom of the embankment when he felt the ground beneath him begin to shake and saw the top of the dam breached by the straining waters. He just had time to scramble up the side before a large section of the dam collapsed, unleashing a solid wall of water down into the valley below towards Sheffield. The torrent destroyed everything in its path and though the waters started to subside within half an hour their destructive force swept aside 415 houses, 106 factories or shops, 20 bridges and countless cottage and market gardens for 8 miles (12.9km). Few were spared and some whole families were wiped out, including an 87-year-old woman and a two-day-old baby.

At the inquest the jury concluded that there had been insufficient engineering skill devoted to a work of such size and called for legislation to ensure 'frequent, sufficient and regular' inspections of dams. The Dale Dike Dam was rebuilt in 1875 but it was not brought into full use until 1887, a very dry year.

WALK 7 DIRECTIONS

1 Exit the car park and turn right on to the road. At the second junction go right towards Midhopestones. Follow this road uphill passing, on the right, a former inn, Walker House farm and Upper Thornseat. When the road turns right, with Thomson House below, turn left on to an overgrown track.

WHILE YOU'RE THERE

Don't miss the Parish Church of St Nicholas, which dates from 1487. It contains a Norman font gifted by the Cistercian monks at Roche Abbey and a Saxon cross found at Low Bradfield in the late 19th century. But it is the Watch House at the gates of the church that sets it apart. Built in 1745 to prevent body snatching it is the last one to survive in Yorkshire.

---

2 From here go through a gate in front of you and on to Hall Lane, a public bridleway. Follow this along the edge of a wood then through another gate and continue ahead on the farm road. Another gate at the end of this road leads to the entrance to Hallfield.

3 The right of way goes through the grounds of Hallfield but

WHAT TO LOOK OUT FOR

A memorial was erected at the dam in 1991 to commemorate those who lost their lives in the flood. It's a simple memorial stone surrounded by a small garden. Next to it there's a white stone bearing the letters CLOB. This is one of four stones that mark the Centre Line of the Old Bank and are the only trace today of where the earthen embankment of the previous dam stood.

WHERE TO EAT AND DRINK

The Plough is more than 200 years old and has held a licence for most of that time. A former farmhouse, it contains an enormous stone hearth, stone walls and traditional timbers. Real ales and traditional home-cooked food is the standard fare.

---

an alternative permissive path leads left through a gate, round the perimeter of the house and through another gate to rejoin the bridleway at the back of the house. Follow the bridleway through a gate and then past Stubbing Farm.

4 The next gate leads to Brogging Farm and the dam at the head of Strines Reservoir. Look out for a sign near the end of the farmhouse and turn left. Go slightly downhill, over a stile, follow the path, then cross a stile and go through a wood.

5 Cross the stream by a footbridge, go right at a junction and straight on at the next with the stream on your left. Then follow the path along the bank of Dale Dike Reservoir to the dam head. From here continue through the woods, down several sets of steps and continue on the path looking out for the memorial to those who were killed in 1864.

6 Follow the path until it reaches the road. Cross the stile, turn right on to the road and proceed to the road junction. Turn right, cross the bridge then look for a public footpath sign just before the entrance to Doe House. Cross the stile on the left and follow the path all the way to it's end on Mill Lee Road opposite The Plough. Turn left and follow this road downhill, through the village and back to the car park.

On the Moorland's Edge

To Lantern Pike and Middle Moor above the Sett Valley above Hayfield.

DISTANCE *7 miles (11.3km)*   **MINIMUM TIME** *4hrs*

ASCENT/GRADIENT *1,640ft (500m)* ▲▲▲ **LEVEL OF DIFFICULTY** ✦✦✦

PATHS *Good paths and tracks, plenty of stiles*

LANDSCAPE *Heather moorland, and rolling farm pastures*

SUGGESTED MAP *OS Explorer OL1 Dark Peak*

START / FINISH *Grid reference: SK 036869*

DOG FRIENDLINESS *Walk is on farmland and access agreement land, dogs should be kept on lead*

PARKING *Sett Valley Trail pay car park, Hayfield*

PUBLIC TOILETS *At car park*

Hayfield was busy. It had cotton mills, papermaking mills and calico printing and dye factories. Hayfield had times of trouble. Floods washed away three bridges, even swept away some bodies from their churchyard graves. And in 1830 it resounded to marching feet of a thousand protesting mill workers, demanding a living wage. As was always the case in such times, the men were beaten back by soldiers and charged with civil disorder. Their industry went into a slow decline that would last a century, and Hayfield returned to its countryside ways.

The Sett Valley Trail

The first part of the walk to little Lantern Pike follows the Sett Valley Trail, the trackbed of a railway that until 1970 linked Manchester and New Mills with Hayfield. At its peak the steam train would have brought thousands of people from Manchester. Today it's a pleasant tree-lined track, working its way through the valley between the hills of Lantern Pike and Chinley Churn. The track, and its former wasteland surroundings, are becoming quite a haven for wildlife. Beneath the ash, sycamore, beech and oak you'll see wood anemone, bluebells and wild garlic along with the rhubarb-like butterbur. In the days before fridges butterbur leaves were used to wrap butter to keep it cool.

Lantern Pike

Lantern Pike is the middle of three ridges peeping through the trees, and by the time you get to Birch Vale you're ready to tackle it. You ascend on a shady path through woods, then a country lane with wild flowers in the verges, and finally on heather and grass slopes to the rocky-crested summit. Lantern Pike's name comes from the beacon tower that once stood on its summit. It had to be demolished in 1907 after falling into a dangerous state of disrepair. Having descended back down to the busy Glossop road the route then climbs up across Middle Moor where it enters a new landscape – one of expansive heather fields. Soon you're on the skyline looking down on the Kinder and the ever-so-green valley beneath your feet. This seems to be complemented to perfection by the shapely and ever-so-green peaks of Mount Famine and South Head.

Into Modern Hayfield

You come down to Hayfield on the Snake Path, an old traders' route linking the Sett and Woodland valleys. A fine street of stone-built cottages, with window boxes overflowing with flowers, takes you to the centre. This is a place where walkers come, and motorists take tea before motoring somewhere else. It's all so very peaceful – now.

WALK 8 DIRECTIONS

❶ Follow the old railway trackbed signed 'The Sett Valley Trail and Pennine Bridleway', from the car park in Hayfield. This heads west down the valley and above the River Sett to meet a minor road close to the A6015 New Mills road at Birch Vale.

❷ Turn right along the road, then right again along a cobbled track behind the cottages of the Crescent into the shade of woods. Beyond a gate, the track meets a tarred farm lane at a hairpin bend. Follow the higher course to reach a country lane. Staggered to the right across it, a surfaced lane climbs further up the hillside. Take the left fork near Upper Cliffe Farm to a gate at the edge of the National Trust's Lantern Pike site.

3 Leave the bridleway here and turn left along a grassy wallside path climbing heather and bracken slopes to the rock-fringed ridge. Turn right and climb the airy crest to Lantern Pike's summit, which is topped by a view indicator.

4 From here, the path continues northwards from the top of Lantern Pike, descending to a gate at the northern boundary of the National Trust estate, where it rejoins the track you left earlier. Follow this northwards across high pastures to a five-way footpath signpost to the west of Blackshaw Farm.

5 Turn left along the walled farm lane past Bullshaw Farm, then right on a track passing the buildings of Matleymoor Farm. Where the track swings to the right leave it for a rough grassy track on the left. Go over the stile at its end and continue northwards on a grooved path, which joins a semi-surfaced track from Knarrs.

6 At the end turn right and walk along the road to reach the A624 road. Cross this with care and go over the stile at the far side. Turn immediately right, following a faint, rutted track with a wall on the right-hand side. This crosses the little valley of Hollingworth Clough on a footbridge before

climbing up the heather slopes of Middle Moor.

7 Near a white shooting cabin, turn right on the stony Snake Path, which descends through heather at first, then, beyond a kissing gate, across fields to reach a stony walled track. Follow it down to Kinder Road near the centre of Hayfield.

8 Turn right down the lane, then left down steps to Church Street. Turn left to St Matthew's Church, then right down a side street signed to the Sett Valley Trail. This leads to the busy main road. Cross with care back to the car park.

In the Footsteps of the Trespass

A dramatic route to Kinder Downfall follows the famous trespassers of 1932.

DISTANCE *8 miles (12.9km)*   **MINIMUM TIME** *5hrs*

ASCENT/GRADIENT *1,450ft (440m)* ▲▲▲   **LEVEL OF DIFFICULTY** +++

PATHS *Well-defined tracks and paths, quite a few stiles*

LANDSCAPE *Heather and peat moorland and farm pastures*

SUGGESTED MAP *OS Explorer OL1 Dark Peak*

START / FINISH *Grid reference: SK 048869*

DOG FRIENDLINESS *Walk is on farmland and access agreement land, dogs should be kept on leads*

PARKING *Bowden Bridge pay car park*

PUBLIC TOILETS *Across bridge from car park*

If you want to climb one of the quieter ways to Kinder Scout, Hayfield to the west is one of the best places to start. It's also a route with a bit of history to it. From the beginning of the 20th century there had been conflict between ramblers and the owners of Kinder's moorland plateau. By 1932 ramblers from the industrial conurbations of Sheffield and Manchester, disgusted by lack of government action to open up the moors to walkers, decided to hold a mass trespass on Kinder Scout. Benny Rothman, a Manchester rambler and a staunch communist, would lead the trespass on Sunday 24 April. The police expected to intercept Benny at Hayfield railway station, but he outwitted them by arriving on his bicycle, not in the village itself, but at Bowden Bridge Quarry to the east. Here he was greeted by hundreds of cheering fellow ramblers. With the police in hot pursuit the group made their way towards Kinder Scout.

Although they were threatened and barracked by a large gathering of armed gamekeepers the ramblers still managed to get far enough to join their fellow trespassers from Sheffield, who had come up from the Snake Inn. Predictably, fighting broke out and Benny Rothman was one of five arrested. He was given a four-month jail sentence for unlawful assembly and breach of the peace. The ramblers' cause inspired folk singer, Ewan McColl (famous for *Dirty Old Town* and *The First Time Ever I Saw Your Face*) to write *The Manchester Rambler*, which became something of an anthem for the proliferating walkers' clubs and societies. However it took until 1951, when the recently formed National Park negotiated access agreements with the landowners, for the situation to improve.

Just like the mass trespass this walk starts at Bowden Bridge, where you will see a commemorative plaque on the rock face above the car park. After climbing through the Kinder Valley and above Kinder Reservoir you're confronted by those same moors of purple heather and the enticing craggy sides of the Scout. But now it is the National Park signs that greet you, not a gun-toting gamekeeper.

The Downfall

A dark shadow-filled cleft in the rocks captures your attention. It's the Kinder Downfall, where the infant Kinder tumbles off the plateau. Now you climb to the edge for the most spectacular part of the walk – the part that would have been a trespass all those years ago – and continue along a promenade of dusky gritstone rock. Round the next corner you come to that dark cleft seen earlier. In the dry summer months the fall is a mere trickle, just enough to wet the rocks, but after the winter rains it can turn into a 100ft (30m) torrent, thrashing against the jumble of boulders below. The prevailing west wind often catches the torrent, funnelling it back up to the top rocks like plumes of white smoke. In contrast, the way down is gentle, leaving the edge at Red Brook and descending the pastures of Tunstead Clough Farm. A quiet leafy lane takes you back into the Kinder Valley.

WALK 9 DIRECTIONS

❶ Turn left out of the car park and walk up the lane, which winds beneath the trees and by the banks of the River Kinder. After 550yds (503m), leave the lane at a signposted footpath after crossing a bridge. Follow the path as it traces the east bank of the river before turning left to rejoin the road at a point just short of the treatment plant buildings.

❷ Here you fork left through a gate on to a cobbled bridleway, climbing above the buildings. It continues alongside the reservoir's north shore, turning sharp left on White Brow. Beyond a gate, but don't cross over the footbridge, follow the path instead as it climbs alongside William Clough, where it is joined by the Snake Path from the left.

3 The path crosses and recrosses the stream as it works its way up the grass and heather clough. In the upper stages the narrowing clough loses its vegetation and the stream becomes a trickle in the peat. Climb to Ashop Head where you meet the Pennine Way at a crossroads of paths.

WHERE TO EAT AND DRINK

Near the car park on Kinder Road, The Sportsman is a walker-friendly pub, which serves hot and cold food every lunchtime and evening – from snacks to main meals. Children and dogs are welcome and there's a pleasant outside seating area.

4 Turn right to walk along the slabbed Pennine Way path across the moor towards Kinder Scout's north-west edge, then climb those last gritstone slopes on a pitched path to gain the summit plateau. Now it's easy walking along the edge.

5 After turning left into the rocky combe of the River Kinder, the Mermaid's Pool and the Kinder Downfall (waterfalls) come into view. Descend to cross the Kinder's shallow rocky channel about 100yds (91m) back from the edge before turning right and continuing along the edge.

6 Beyond Red Brook, leave the plateau by taking the right fork, which descends south westwards, contouring round grassy slopes beneath the rocky edge.

WHAT TO LOOK OUT FOR

When you're absorbed in the cerebral pleasures of wilderness walking, some comic bird with a flash of red on his head will probably wreck the moment by cackling loudly before scuttling from under your feet. This red grouse will have been absorbed in the pleasures of the tasty heather shoots you are passing. The gamekeeper makes sure that this ungainly bird has all he needs to breed successfully – a mixture of young heather and mature plants for cover.

7 After passing The Three Knolls rocks and swinging right beneath the slopes of Kinderlow End, go through a gate in a fence (grid reference 066867) before taking a right fork to reach another gate in the wall dividing the moor and farmland. Go over a stile next to it and then turn left through a gateway. Descend the trackless pastured spur, passing through several gates and stiles at the field boundaries to pass to the left of Tunstead Clough Farm.

8 Turn right beyond the farmhouse to follow a winding track that descends into the upper Sett Valley. At the crossroads of lanes at the bottom, go straight ahead, and along the road to emerge at Bowden Bridge.

WHILE YOU'RE THERE

In 2007, the 75th anniversary of the mass trespass was marked by the opening of the Trespass Trail, a 14-mile (22.6km) walk following the route of the original brave trespassers up on to Kinder Scout. A booklet guide is available from Hayfield Information Centre.

Right: View from Kinder Downfall, Peak District National Park (Walk 9)

Pennine Ways on Kinder Scout

One end of the famous long distance trail ascends to the craggy outcrops of the Kinder Plateau.

DISTANCE 5 miles (8km)   **MINIMUM TIME** 3hrs 30min
ASCENT/GRADIENT 1,650ft (500m) ▲▲▲   **LEVEL OF DIFFICULTY** +++
PATHS Rock and peat paths, some steep and rough
LANDSCAPE Heather moor
SUGGESTED MAP OS Explorer OL1 Dark Peak
START / FINISH Grid reference: SK 125853
DOG FRIENDLINESS Walk is on farmland and access agreement land, dogs should be kept on leads
PARKING Edale pay car park
PUBLIC TOILETS At car park

Edale sits peacefully in a paradise of pasture, riverside meadow and hedgerow, surrounded by high peaks. Its church spire towers above the cottages and farmhouses of its five scattered booths, but is in turn dwarfed by the castellated crags of Kinder Scout, and the rounded hills of the Mam Tor ridge.

Rambling Man
In depression torn 1930s England, Tom Stephenson, then secretary of the Ramblers' Association, told the readers of the *Daily Herald* of his dream – to create a long, green trail across the roof of England. This dream would bring Edale to the world's attention. It took 30 years, a mass trespass and Acts of Parliament to achieve, but in 1965, the Pennine Way was opened. Spanning over 250 miles (405km) from Edale to Kirk Yetholm in Scotland it was Britain's first official long distance trail. Go to Edale any Friday night and you'll see eager-eyed Pennine Wayfarers. They'll be in the campsite making their last minute preparations, or in the Old Nags Head poring over Ordnance Survey maps or looking though Wainwright's little green guidebook.

Popular Trail
Unfortunately the popularity of the Way has led to the main route through Grindsbrook being diverted along the foul weather route up Jacob's Ladder. But as you leave Edale, or to be more strictly correct Grindsbrook Booth (Edale is the name of the valley), you can look across to the old route, which delves deep into the rocky ravine. Your route climbs boldly to the top of Ringing Roger (the echoing rocks). From this great viewpoint you can look down on the length of Edale and across to the great Lose Hill–Mam Tor ridge. What follows is an edge walk round the great chasm of Grindsbrook, taking you past Nether Tor to the place where the old Pennine Way track comes to meet you. The Way didn't bother with the comforts of the edge, but got stuck into those peat hags to the right. It was a stiff navigational challenge to get to the Kinder Downfall on the other side of the expansive plateau. Past weather-smoothed gritstone sculptures and the rocky peak of Grindslow Knoll you

Left: Edale, Peak District National Park (Walk 11)

come to another ravine, that of Crowden Brook. This route descends by the brook, passing several waterfalls and offering many chances for a paddle to cool those feet. Beneath the open slopes the path seeks the shade of recently planted pine, larch, birch and oak. Colourful wild flowers, including bluebells, daffodils and primroses, proliferate in this delightful spot, just above Upper Booth. Finally you're reacquainted with the Pennine Way, following the new route back across the fields of Edale.

WALK 10 DIRECTIONS

1 Turn right out of the car park and head north along the lane into Edale village, under the railway and past The Old Nags Head. At the end, turn right and follow the path across the footbridge over Grinds Brook.

2 Leave the main Grindsbrook Clough path by the side of a barn, taking the right fork that climbs up the lower hillslope to a stile on the edge of open country. Beyond the stile the path zig-zags above Fred Heardman's Plantation then climbs up the nose of The Nab to the skyline rocks. Where the path divides, take the right fork to the summit of Ringing Roger.

3 Follow the edge path left, rounding the cavernous hollow of Grindsbrook past Nether Tor. The old Pennine Way route is met on the east side by a large cairn.

4 Ignoring the left fork heading for the outlier of Grindslow Knoll, follow the paved footpath westwards to the head of another deep hollow, the clough of Crowden Brook.

5 Cross over Crowden Brook, and then immediately leave the edge to follow a narrow level path traversing slopes on the left beneath the imposing outcrop of Crowden Tower. Below the tower, fork left for a steep and, at first, rough track down to the banks of

the brook. The path now follows the brook, fording the path on several occasions.

6 Cross a stile at the edge of open country and then go across a footbridge shaded by tall rowans to change to the west bank. From here the path threads through woodland before descending in steps to the road at Upper Booth. You now need to follow the Pennine Way path back to Edale.

7 Turn left along the road and then left again into the farmyard of Upper Booth Farm before exiting at the top right corner. After following a track to a gateway, bear left uphill to a stile by an old barn. Here the Way traverses fields at the foot of Broadlee Bank before joining a tree-lined track into the village. Turn right along the road back to the car park.

EXTENDING THE WALK

You can extend this walk from Point **5**, continuing along the edge of the Kinder plateau, then descending to Upper Booth on the Pennine Way route by Jacob's Ladder to then rejoin the main walk at Point **7**.

WHAT TO LOOK OUT FOR
Along the edge of Kinder Scout's summit are peat bogs. Peat is formed by mosses such as the bright green sphagnum moss, which is now restricted to small patches. It has been replaced by sedges, grasses, heather and bilberry in a vegetation cover riven by deep and numerous hags in which the naked peat comes to the surface. The base of the hag has often been eroded to the gravelly surface of the core rocks. There are many reasons for this. The chief factors have been grazing and pollution.

Mysterious Mam Tor and Rushup Edge

Approaching from the Edale side, discover the ancient secrets of the great 'Shivering Mountain'.

WALK 11

DISTANCE 6 miles (9.7km) **MINIMUM TIME** 3hrs 30min

ASCENT/GRADIENT 984ft (300m) ▲▲▲ **LEVEL OF DIFFICULTY** +++

PATHS Mainly good but can be boggy in wet weather

LANDSCAPE Woodland, hills and meadows

SUGGESTED MAP OS Explorer OL1 Dark Peak

START / FINISH Grid reference: SK 124853

DOG FRIENDLINESS Suitable for dogs, but keep on lead near livestock

PARKING Edale pay car park

PUBLIC TOILETS At car park

With its spectacular views and close proximity to the road it's hardly surprising that Mam Tor is the most popular of the Peak District hill-forts. Unfortunately this popularity has resulted in the National Trust having to pave the footpath and a large area around the summit to prevent serious erosion.

The 'Shivering Mountain'

Called the Shivering Mountain because of the instability of its shale layers, Mam Tor is the largest of the Peak's hill-forts and has the distinction of being the only one to be excavated. In the mid-1960s Manchester University selected Mam Tor as a training site for its archaeology students and this produced a wealth of fresh information about the fort.

What can be seen today are the ramparts of a heavily fortified Iron Age settlement. The single rampart with an outer ditch and another bank can still be traced round the hillside. There were two entrances, one leading to the path from Hollins Cross and the other to the path to Mam Nick. Mam Tor was probably a partially defended site with a timber palisade that was later replaced with stone.

Ancient Settlement

The excavations revealed that there had been a settlement here long before the Iron Age. Two Early Bronze Age barrows were discovered on the summit, one of which the National Trust has capped in stone to make sure it is preserved. An earlier settlement on the ground enclosed by the ramparts was excavated. Here several circular houses or huts had been built on terraced platforms on the upper slopes of the hill. The pottery and other artefacts uncovered are of a style often found in house platforms of this type and date from the Late Bronze Age. Radiocarbon dating of charcoal found in the huts put them somewhere between 1700 and 1000 BC.

Archaeologists, G D B Jones and F H Thomson, writing about the discoveries at Mam Tor, suggested that the fort might have been built as a shelter for pastoralists using the hills for summer grazing, but decided in the end that it was more likely to have had a strategic military purpose. Depending on when it was actually built, it could have seen action during inter-tribal struggles of the native Brigantes. It may well at a later period have been used as a strategic defence against the advancing Romans. Like most settlements from this far back in time Mam Tor will probably never reveal all its secrets, but standing on the summit and looking away down the valleys on either side, back along the path to Hollins Cross or forward to Rushup Edge it's enough just to try and imagine the effort that went into building such an enormous fortification with nothing but the most primitive of tools.

WALK 11 DIRECTIONS

❶ Exit the car park at Edale and turn right on to the main road. Look out for a public footpath sign on the left and turn on to a farm road. Just before this road turns sharply left, take the public footpath that forks off to the right and goes uphill through a wood.

❷ At the end of the wooded area cross over a stile and then continue walking uphill. Go across another stile, follow the path across open hillside, then cross yet another stile and turn left on to the road. Just before the road bends sharply left, cross the road, go over a stile and follow this path towards a hill.

WALK 11

3 Near the foot of the hill cross over a stile to the left and turn right on to the road. Continue to find the steps on the left leading through the ramparts of an Iron Age fort to the summit of Mam Tor. From here trace your steps back to the road.

4 Cross the road, go over a stile and continue on the footpath uphill and on to Rushup Edge. Follow this well-defined path along the ridge crossing five stiles. When the path is intersected by another, go right. This is Chapel Gate track, badly eroded in places.

WHILE YOU'RE THERE

The ruins of Peveril Castle at nearby Castleton are well enough preserved to give a good indication of what it looked like when it was intact. Its glorious clifftop location also gives grand views in all directions. It was built by William Peveril in 1080 after he was granted the title of Bailiff of the Royal Manors of the Peak by William I for his part in the Norman Conquest of 1066.

5 Near the bottom of the hill go through a gap stile on the left. Go across another stile, then through a gate and across yet another stile on the left. This leads to some tumbledown buildings. Cross a stile by the corner of one building and then veer right to cross another stile on to a farm road.

6 Cross the road, go through a gate and then follow the path until it joins a road. Turn right and then left at the junction and into Barber Booth. Take the second turn on the left on a tarmac lane, then, near the outskirts of the village, turn left on a road signposted to Edale Station.

WHAT TO LOOK OUT FOR

On your return to Edale make sure to leave enough time to visit the fascinating Moorland Centre, opened by the Peak District National Park in 2006. Featuring interactive displays and exhibitions on ecology and wildlife of the Dark Peak moorland, the centre also provides a wet weather shelter and toilets and has daily weather reports for walkers. Free to enter, the state-of-the-art building has a sedum roof and is heated by a ground source heat pump.

7 Follow the path across fields, forking right after Shaw Wood Farm. Finally you emerge on a road next to Champion House. Turn left to visit the Moorland Centre (100yds/91m), right to the car park.

WHERE TO EAT AND DRINK

Head for the Hikers Bar at The Old Nags Head in Edale. Built in 1577 it has been the official start of the Pennine Way since 1965. There's an excellent selection of good hot food, a list of tasty specials as well as several well-kept ales as well as tea and coffee. As the name suggests, muddy boots and walkers are not a problem here.

Marching Roads and Battlefields

Following the ancient roads over Win Hill to the Roman fort at Navio, via the site of an ancient battle.

DISTANCE *8.75 miles (14.1km)*   MINIMUM TIME *5hrs*

ASCENT/GRADIENT *1,050ft (320m)* ▲▲▲   LEVEL OF DIFFICULTY +++

PATHS *Paths can be slippery after rain, quite a few stiles*

LANDSCAPE *Riverside pastureland and high peak*

SUGGESTED MAP *OS Explorer OL1 Dark Peak*

START / FINISH *Grid reference: SK 149829*

DOG FRIENDLINESS *Dogs should be kept on lead, except on lanes*

PARKING *Main Castleton pay car park*

PUBLIC TOILETS *At car park*

Leaving Castleton beneath Peveril Castle's Norman keep sets the scene for a walk through history. You're treading the same ground as Roman soldiers and Celtic and Saxon warriors before you. The walk takes you on to the hillside beyond the sycamores of the River Noe. As you amble across green pastures overlooking the Hope Valley, cast your imagination back to the darker days of AD 926. Down there in the valley below you, a furious tribal battle ended in victory for King Athelstan, grandson of Alfred the Great. He would soon become the first Saxon ruler of all England.

Navio – a Roman Fort

In one of those riverside fields the path comes across the earthwork remains of the Roman fort, Navio. Built in the time of Emperor Antoninus Pius, the fort stood at a junction of roads serving garrisons at Buxton, Glossop, and Templeborough. At its peak it would have sheltered over 500 soldiers. It remained occupied until the 4th century, controlling the rich mining area around the Peak. Many Roman relics found near the fort can be viewed at the Buxton Museum.

Win Hill looms large in your thoughts as you cross to the other side of the valley and climb towards it. As you're passing through the hamlet of Aston take a quick look at Aston Hall. Built in 1578, it has an unusual pedimented window with a weather-worn carved figure. The doorway is surrounded by Roman Doric columns and a four-centred arch.

Beyond the hall the climb begins in earnest up a stony track, then through bracken and grass hillside where Win Hill's rocky summit peeps out across the heathered ridge. A concrete trig point caps the rocks. And what a view to reward your efforts! The Ladybower Reservoir's sinuous shorelines creep between dark spruce woods, while the gritstone tors of Kinder Scout, the Derwent Edge, and Bleaklow fill the northern horizon, framed by the pyramidal Lose Hill.

There are several theories on how Win Hill got its name. The most likely one is that it derives from an earlier name, Wythinehull, which meant Willow Hill. The one I prefer though concerns two warlords, Edwin, the first Christian king of Northumbria, and Cuicholm, King of Wessex. Cuicholm murdered Lilla, Edwin's maidservant, and Edwin was looking for revenge. Cuicholm assembled his forces on Lose Hill, while his enemy camped on Win Hill. Edwin was victorious and thus his hill was named Win Hill. Now you follow Edwin down the hill, before continuing across the Hope Valley fields back to Castleton.

WALK 12 DIRECTIONS

1 Turn left out of the car park along the main street. At the far end of the village turn right on a walled stony lane and continue along a well-defined path accompanying Peakshole Water. Cross the railway with care and continue along the path to its end at Pindale Road.

2 Turn left here, then right at the next junction. After 200yds (183m), go over a stile by a gate on the left and follow the path running roughly parallel to the lane at first, then the River Noe, to reach the site of the Roman fort of Navio. Beyond the earthworks go over a stile in a fence and bear half right across another field to reach the B6049 road at Brough.

3 Turn left through the village and cross the footbridge over the River Noe. Go left over a stile and head north-west to the A6187. Turn left along the road for 200yds (183m) to a small gate just beyond a cottage. Follow the hedge and dyke on the right to pass to the right of some houses.

4 Turn left along the lane heading towards the railway station, then go right along a narrow path, which leads to a footbridge over the line. Cross the bridge and turn right at its far end, then left over a stile to cross yet more fields, this time keeping the fence on your right.

5 When you reach Aston turn left along the road, then almost immediately turn right along a narrow, surfaced lane, signposted 'To Win Hill and Hope Cross'.

6 Beyond Edge Farm an unsurfaced track on the left takes the route along the top edge of some woods to a path junction above Twitchill Farm. Now climb right on a well-used path to Win Hill's summit.

7 From the summit retrace your steps back to the junction above Twitchill Farm. This time descend left past the farm on a tarmac drive, to the railway.

8 Turn left under the railway tunnel for the lane via Kilhill Bridge to Edale Road. Turn right along the road, under the railway bridge, then turn left by a red post box on a field path.

9 By a cottage turn right on a path climbing towards Lose Hill. Take the left fork, which is signposted 'Castleton' to follow a waymarked route westwards to Spring House Farm.

10 In front of the farm, turn right to walk along a track behind Losehill Hall. Where the lane swings left, leave it to follow a cross-field path, which joins a rough lane. After passing the outdoor centre, turn left along Hollowford Road into Castleton.

SHORTENING THE WALK

If you want a shorter walk, without the climb up to Win Hill, you can still get reasonable views if you start the walk in Hope and join the main route at Point **2** Leave it again at Point **A**, near Twitchill Farm, and follow the raking path up to Wooler Knoll, with fine views over Ladybower Reservoir. Clear tracks lead back into the valley by Fullwood Stile Farm and Edale Road, from where you can pick out field tracks taking you back to Hope.

Castles and Caverns

Castleton is where the limestone of the White Peak and the shales and gritstone of the Dark Peak collide.

DISTANCE 5 miles (8km) MINIMUM TIME 3hrs

ASCENT/GRADIENT 820ft (250m) ▲▲▲ LEVEL OF DIFFICULTY +++

PATHS Path below Blue John Mines can be tricky in wintry conditions

LANDSCAPE Limestone ravines and high pastureland

SUGGESTED MAP OS Explorer OL1 Dark Peak

START / FINISH Grid reference: SK 149829

DOG FRIENDLINESS Farmland, dogs should be kept on lead

PARKING Main Castleton pay car park by visitor centre

PUBLIC TOILETS At car park

Castleton is the last settlement before the Hope Valley narrows and squeezes into the rocky ravine of Winnats. It's a bustling tourist town with a history evident back to Norman times, and a geology that has been responsible for many of its successes and most of its failures.

At Castleton the shales and gritstone of the Dark Peak and the limestone plateaux of the White Peak meet. Here countless generations of miners have dug their shafts and enlarged the natural caves which riddle the bedrock in search of precious ore. Here too, they built an ambitious road that eventually succumbed to the landslides of Mam Tor, the 'Shivering Mountain'. The castle keep is perched high upon an outcrop of limestone. It's one of the earliest stone-built castles in the country, built shortly after the Norman Conquest by William Peveril, William the Conqueror's illegitimate son.

Dramatic Cave Dale

The entrance to Cave Dale is narrow and dramatic. One minute you're in the village square, the next you've turned the corner and entered an awesome limestone ravine. Geologists used to think Cave Dale was a collapsed cavern, but current thinking places it as a valley carved by glaciers of the last Ice Age.

A little limestone path takes you through the ravine, climbing past cave entrances and over the tops of a wide system of subterranean passages, including those of the nearby Peak Cavern. The valley shallows and the next stretch of the journey is over high green fields enclosed by dry-stone walls. Mam Tor, the Shivering Mountain, dominates the view ahead and soon you look down on the crumbling tarmac of the ill-fated road, and the huge shale landslides that have plagued the valley for centuries.

The first Castleton cavern of the day is the superb Blue John Mine, high on the side of Mam Tor. It takes its name from the purple-blue fluorspar, unique to Castleton. The floodlights of the chambers show off the old river galleries with crystalline waterfalls, and a fascinating array of stalagmites and stalactites.

Boat Trips

Beyond the Blue John Mine a narrow path rakes across the steep limestone-studded slopes past Treak Cliff Cavern to the Speedwell Cavern, at the foot of the Winnats Pass. If you like boat trips, a visit to this cavern is a must. Here, lead miners excavated a level into the hill, through which they built a subterranean canal, 547yds (500m) long. This took them 11 years, but low yields and high costs forced the early closure of the mine. The fascinating boat trip takes you down the canal to a landing stage just short of the 'Bottomless Pit', named because the spoil thrown in by miners made no impression on its depth.

The last stretch takes you across the National Trust's Longcliffe Estate. Before retreating to Castleton, take one last look back up the valley, and across the limestone that was once a coral reef in a tropical lagoon.

WALK 13 DIRECTIONS

❶ From the car park turn left to go down the main street and then turn right to walk along Castle Street, passing the church and the youth hostel on your way.

❷ On reaching the Market Place, turn left to Bar Gate, where a signpost points to Cave Dale. Through a gate, the path enters the limestone gorge with the ruined keep of Peveril Castle perched on the cliffs to the right.

3 As you gain height the gorge shallows. Go through a gate in the dry-stone wall and follow the well-defined track across high pastureland. It passes through a gate in another wall before being joined by a path that has descended the grassy hillside on the right. The track divides soon after the junction. Take the left fork, which climbs uphill, slightly away from the wall on the right to the top corner of the field. Go through the gate here and follow a short stretch of walled track to a crossroads of routes near the old Hazard Mine.

4 Turn right beyond the gate here to walk along a stony walled lane, which swings right to reach a minor road near Oxlow House Farm. Take the path across the road to the disused quarry on Windy Knoll.

5 At the quarry turn right on a grassy footpath to a minor road. After turning left to the next junction, take the old Mam Tor Road (straight ahead).

6 After 400yds (366m) turn right down the tarmac approach road to Blue John Cavern, then left by the ticket office. Go through the gate and trace the path as it crosses several fields. Beyond a gate the path arcs to the right, traversing the now steep grassy hillslopes. It passes Treak Cliff Cavern ticket office. Go left down the concrete steps by the ticket office, then right on a concrete path with handrails.

7 Half-way down, take the hillside path on the right, signposted 'Winnats Pass'. On the approach to Speedwell Cavern the path becomes indistinct, but there's an obvious stile straight ahead which will take you out on to the Winnats road.

8 A path on the far side of the road takes the route through the National Trust's Longcliff Estate. It roughly follows the line of a wall and veers left beneath the hillslopes of Cow Low to reach Goosehill Hall. Here, follow Goosehill (a lane), back into Castleton. Beyond Goosehill Bridge, turn left down a surfaced streamside path to the car park.

Alport's Castles in the Clouds

From historic Fairholmes in the Derwent Valley up to the towering rocky pinnacles of Alport Castles.

DISTANCE 8 miles (12.9km)   **MINIMUM TIME** 5hrs 30min

ASCENT/GRADIENT 2,000ft (610m) ▲▲▲ **LEVEL OF DIFFICULTY** +++

PATHS Well-defined paths and tracks in forests and on moorland

LANDSCAPE Afforested hillsides and peaty moorland

SUGGESTED MAP OS Explorer OL1 Dark Peak

START / FINISH Grid reference: SK 173893

DOG FRIENDLINESS Much of the walk is across farmland and access agreement land, dogs should be kept on lead

PARKING Fairholmes pay car park

PUBLIC TOILETS At car park

The walk begins in the Derwent Valley, beneath the great stone ramparts of the impressive Derwent Dam. Fairholmes car park has a history all of its own. At the south end the crumbling foundations of Fairholmes Farm are an evocative reminder that this was once agricultural land. During the construction of the reservoirs the upper car park was a masons' yard reverberating to the sounds of workmen cutting, shaping and dressing stone for the dams. The stone came from the Longshaw quarry and was transported here by a specially constructed railway, which linked with the LMS sidings in Bamford.

England's Largest Landslip

You don't stay long in the valley – the route has higher things in mind, and climbs through Lockerbrook Coppice. After emerging from the trees, the route follows the top edge of the vast Hagg Side spruce plantation before climbing to Bellhag Tor. Here you get the first view of the landslips that have occurred in the region. However, by climbing north-west along the peaty ridge of Rowlee Pasture, England's largest landslip will be revealed beneath your feet. They call it Alport Castles and, as you stand on the edge of the cliff looking across to the Tower, you can see why. A huge gritstone tor towers above a chaotic jumble of tumbled boulders and the grassy mounds that have been separated from the main ridge. The reason for the instability lies in the shales that are squeezed between the tiers of gritstone here. In wetter times, after the last Ice Age, the river eroded these soft bands, resulting in a half-mile (800m) long landslide that dropped 100ft (30m) below the main cliff.

Secret Lovefeast

Looking across the Castle your eye is led to the great straw-coloured expanses of Bleaklow, but we'll save that for another day. Your route takes you on a little path beneath the gritstone walls and down towards Alport Castles Farm in the valley below. On the first Sunday of every July they

WALK 14

hold the Woodlands Lovefeast service in the barn. These non-conformist religious ceremonies started during the reign of Charles II. Presbyterianism in such times was against the law, and the services had to be held in remote places, far from the eyes of the King's loyal subjects.

Past the farm you follow the valley to its meeting with the Ashop Valley. Here an old Roman road that linked forts at Melandra, at Glossop, and Navio, near Bradwell, takes you across the lower grassy slopes of Kinder Scout, where a jaggers' track is waiting to take you down to a secluded little packhorse bridge at Haggwater before transporting you over the hill towards Fairholmes.

WALK 14 DIRECTIONS

❶ Leave the car park for the road, then follow a forestry track, signposted to 'Lockerbrook and Derwent Discovery Walk'. It climbs through Hagg Side Wood, crossing the bridge over a water

leat before steepening on the higher slopes. Near the top the waymarked path leaves the forest in sight of the farm.

❷ An obvious footpath, guided by a stone wall, traverses the fields of Lockerbrook Heights. Turn left at a public footpath signpost and follow a track southwards past Lockerbrook Farm.

3 On reaching the ridgetop by Woodcock Coppice, turn right along a permissive path climbing to the open moor at Bellhag Tor.

4 Continue over Rowlee Pasture and along a ridgetop path climbing to Alport Castles.

5 Descend on the good path at the southern end of the Castles. Initially the path follows an old wall. On the lower slopes it traces the perimeter of Castles Wood.

6 Cross the footbridge over the River Alport, where the path turns right. Follow the waymarks across a small field. At Alport Farm turn left on the farm drive and then head southwards down the valley.

7 Where the track veers right for Hayridge Farm, leave it for a signed path descending south-east towards the edge of a small riverside wood, to exit on the busy A57 Snake Road. Across the road follow a stony track to the River Ashop, then cross the footbridge to the right of a ford. Rejoin the track, which skirts the hill slopes beneath Upper Ashop Farm before climbing steadily

across the rough grassy slopes of Blackley Hey. Ignore the left fork (surfaced drive) descending to Rowlee Bridge, but continue with the track you're on as far as the path intersection to the east of Crookstone Barn.

8 Turn left here on the rutted track along the top edge of the pinewoods before entering them. Leave the track just beyond a right-hand bend and follow a narrow path to Haggwater Bridge.

9 Beyond the bridge, the path climbs up again to the A57 Snake Road. Cross the road and join the track opposite. It climbs out of the Woodlands Valley to the east of Hagg Farm and zig-zags across the upper slopes at the edge of Woodcock Coppice before skirting the Hagg Side conifer plantations. Here, retrace your route down through Lockerbrook Coppice to the car park.

A High Ridge and Lost Villages at Ladybower

Beneath the beauty of the Ladybower Reservoir lie the remains of the old village of Ashopton.

DISTANCE 5.5 miles (8.8km)   **MINIMUM TIME** 3hrs 30min

ASCENT/GRADIENT 1,200ft (365m) ▲▲▲   **LEVEL OF DIFFICULTY** +++

PATHS Well-defined moorland paths and a reservoir road

LANDSCAPE High gritstone moorland

SUGGESTED MAP OS OL1 Dark Peak

START / FINISH Grid reference: SK 195864

DOG FRIENDLINESS Keep on lead on access agreement land, could run free by reservoir shores

PARKING Marked lay-by east of Ashopton Viaduct (A57)

PUBLIC TOILETS Heatherdene car park (A6013)

In the north-east corner of Derbyshire, the heather ridges and gritstone tors of Derwent Edge make one last stand before declining to the plains of Yorkshire. It's always been a sparsely populated corner of the country with few references in the history books. Hereabouts, the stories lie beneath the water.

Before the Second World War Ashopton, which lay at the confluence of the rivers Derwent and Ashop, was a huddle of stone-built cottages, a small inn and a blacksmith's shop. A little lane ambled from Ashopton northwards to its neighbouring village, Derwent, which enjoyed an even quieter location in the Upper Derwent valley. But the building of a huge reservoir, the third in the region, shattered the locals' lives. After the completion of its dam in 1943 Ladybower Reservoir gradually filled up, and by 1946 the water level had risen above the rooftops.

Haunting Remains

Before you set off gaze, out at the huge concrete viaduct over the reservoir. Wherever you look there is water. You take a winding track up the next hill, now shaded by a sombre plantation of spruce. The cottages you see here are all that remain of the village of Ashopston. Soon you're through the woods and heading across open moor to the weathered gritstone tors that top the ridge. The rocks of Whinstone Lee Tor are set into a thick carpet of heather. Though the highest hills in the region lie to the north, this is one of the best viewpoints, as the ridge is at its narrowest here. In the west, Kinder Scout's expansive flat top peeps over Crook Hill's rocky crest. In the valley down below, the dark waters of the reservoir still keep their secrets.

After passing the Hurkling Stones, the route descends towards the lakeshore in search of Derwent village. The old gateposts of Derwent Hall still survive by the roadside. A notice board shows the positions of the hall itself, along with the post office, school, church and some of the old cottages. After a dry spell the water level can sometimes fall sufficiently for you to see the crumbling walls and foundations of the village surrounded by

LADYBOWER RESERVOIR

the crazed drying mud. One small bridge is almost intact, but the villagers dismantled the main twin-arched packhorse bridge for rebuilding beyond the reach of the rising water at Slippery Stones, higher up the valley.

Leaving the old village behind you return by the shores of the reservoir. Nature has readjusted. The landscape, though more regimented now, is still beautiful; kestrels still scour the hillside for prey, and dippers frequent the streams as they always have done.

WALK 15 DIRECTIONS

1 Cross over the road and then take the public bridleway following a private road that zig-zags past a few of Ashopton's remaining cottages.

2 The gated road becomes unsurfaced and where it ends double back left on a forestry track climbing through pines and larches. The track emerges from the forest on to Lead Hill, where Ladybower Reservoir and the rather sombre sprawl of Bleaklow come into view.

> ### WHERE TO EAT AND DRINK
> The nearest pub is Ladybower Inn, a short way east along the A57. Slightly further afield you could relax in the Castle at Castleton. This is a 17th-century coaching inn with oak beams and warming open fires in the winter.

3 The path keeps the intake wall to the left as it rakes up the bracken slopes of Lead Hill. Follow the well-worn path as it veers away from the wall up to the ridge. At the junction of paths at the top go second left for the summit of Whistone Lee Tor.

4 The path continues along the peaty ridge past the Hurkling Stones to an unnamed summit. Beyond this it meets a signposted

> ### WHILE YOU'RE THERE
> Visit Derwent and Howden Reservoir dams. Park in Fairholmes car park, south of the Derwent Dam. The dams, built between 1912 and 1916, were used in training forays by the Dambusters of 617 Squadron in preparation for their attacks on the Moehne and Eder dams in 1943.

> ### WHAT TO LOOK FOR
> The mountain hare is quite common on the moortops. It serves as a reminder of the upland nature of this landscape. In winter it's coat changes to a dirty white, to blend with the snow. When there is no snow, it appears faintly ridiculous.

path heading from Ladybower over to Moscar. Descend left until you reach a gate at the edge of the open hillside.

5 Through the gate the path descends westwards and alongside the top wall of a conifer plantation. It fords Grindle Clough's stream beyond another gate and turns past several stone-built barns. The path, now paved, descends further to join the track running along the east shores of Ladybower Reservoir.

6 It's worth a detour here to see the fascinating remains of Derwent village, 400yds (366m) along the track, at the foot of the Mill Brook clough. Retrace your steps along the well-graded track, by the shores of the reservoir. After rounding Grainfoot Clough the track passes beneath woodlands with Whinstone Lee Tor crowning the hilltop.

7 It meets the outward route at a gate above the Ashopton viaduct, opposite the lay-by on the A57 above the reservoir.

EXTENDING THE WALK

You can extend this walk if you choose, by walking across the moorland edges from Point **4** to Dovestone Tor and Back Tor, then descend to Derwent Reservoir and follow the shore of the reservoir to rejoin the main walk at Point **6**.

Following in the Steps of Mr Darcy

A circuit of the attractive grounds of Lyme Park, one of the Peak's finest country houses.

> **DISTANCE** 5.5 miles (8.8km) **MINIMUM TIME** 3hrs 30min
>
> **ASCENT/GRADIENT** 950ft (290m) ▲▲▲ **LEVEL OF DIFFICULTY** ✦✦✦
>
> **PATHS** Generally firm, field tracks can be slippery if wet, a few stiles
>
> **LANDSCAPE** Rolling parkland and fields, some moorland
>
> **SUGGESTED MAP** OS Explorer OL1 Dark Peak
>
> **START / FINISH** Grid reference: SJ 964823
>
> **DOG FRIENDLINESS** On lead in deer sanctuary and around livestock
>
> **PARKING** Lyme Park, off A6 (free to National Trust members)
>
> **PUBLIC TOILETS** By Old Workshop Coffee Shop, near main car park

It's the classic English stately home: a medieval manor house that was gradually transformed into a large and elegant Palladian mansion, and which is today full of antique furniture and tapestries, carvings and clocks. Outside, there are formal gardens (including an Edwardian Rose Garden and an Orangery), plus 1,400 acres (567ha) of gorgeous open moorland and parkland that is home to herds of red and fallow deer.

Such is the sheer magnetism of the place that it was chosen to be the location of Pemberley for BBC Television's adaptation of Jane Austen's *Pride and Prejudice* in 1994, and the sight of a semi-naked Mr Darcy (played by Colin Firth) striding across the grounds apparently remains indelibly printed on many minds.

Magnificent Parkland

Lyme Park was originally created by Richard II who, in 1398, granted land in the Royal Forest of Macclesfield. It became the ancestral home of the Legh family for the next five and a half centuries, and they were responsible for developing the original house into the sumptuous pile that you see today.

In 1946 the house and park were donated to the National Trust who now receive financial support from Stockport Metropolitan Borough Council to manage the estate. The grounds are open all year and the lovely rolling parkland and moorland tracks with their fabulous views over Cheshire and the Dark Peak are well worth exploring.

Near Pursefield Wood is the 300-year-old Paddock Cottage, which was built partly to enhance the radiating views visitors enjoyed to and from the main house. A few of these so-called vista lines, all carefully plotted so that the house can be admired from surrounding locations, are still visible today, including one impressive corridor through the trees of Knightslow Wood to the south of the house.

Other eye-catching buildings include the various lodges that are dotted around the park's perimeter, including Parkgate Lodge. This was once known as the Dower House and was where the widowed mothers of the Lords of the Manor would be expected to reside.

Although the house is often hidden by the undulating moorland, and dense patches of woodland, this walk offers ever-changing views of Lyme Park. From tree-lined avenues and open meadows to the tiny reservoirs of the Bollinhurst Valley. The rough moors to the south and east offer the best vantage points – it is said you can see seven counties from the top of Sponds Hill – but don't forget to examine things closer to hand. Near Bowstonegate is a small enclosure containing the Bow Stones, thought to be the middle sections of late-Saxon crosses. The sole surviving cross head is now to be found in the courtyard at Lyme Park.

WALK 16 DIRECTIONS

❶ With the lake on your right-hand side and the house on your left, leave the car park by the drive and, as it begins to bend to the right, turn left for a wide track to go through a gate signposted 'Gritstone Trail'. Follow this through Knightslow Wood, through several gates, until you emerge on moorland.

LYME PARK

2 Go straight ahead/left on the main track as it climbs the moorland, aiming for the small TV masts on the skyline. At the top cross a stile and a short field to emerge at the end of a surfaced lane by the Bow Stones.

WHAT TO LOOK FOR

The curious hilltop folly known as The Cage is one of Lyme Park's most visible landmarks. An elegant three-storey building, it was built around 1735 as a banqueting house, but since then has been used as an observation tower, as a lodging for the park's gamekeepers, and even as a temporary prison for poachers. After falling derelict it has recently undergone restoration and is occasionally open.

3 Turn left and follow the lane downhill until you reach its junction with another road, opposite the driveway to a hotel. Turn left and walk up the drive of Cock Knoll Farm. When you get to the buildings head right, across the farmyard, as indicated by footpath signs. At the far side go through a gate and down the left-hand side of a field.

4 As you draw level with a small thicket in the shallow valley on the left, go over a stile and through the trees. Out on the other side head right, across the bottom of a field. Clear waymarks now point you through several rough fields to a walled lane on the far side.

5 Once you're on the lane turn right and continue over Bollinhurst Bridge. (If you turn left you can take a short cut back to the house via East Lodge.) Beyond Macclesfield Borough's newly planted Millennium Wood you reach a junction of tracks. Go through the gate on the left

WHERE TO EAT AND DRINK

The Ale Cellar Restaurant inside the house serves a range of 'traditional meals and historic menus' and is licensed, while the Old Workshop Coffee Shop, located near the car park by the large millpond and open daily in season, operates on a self-service basis and has a decent range of snacks and light refreshments.

and take a grassy track, half left, signed to North Lodge.

6 Descend the right-hand side of a rough field to the woodlands at the bottom. The path now goes over several stiles as it skirts round Bollinhurst Reservoir – keep close to the wall on your left. A newly waymarked, gated path takes you around the side of Cockhead Farm, and then continues across another field and down a shaded gravel lane. At the end of the lane turn right, on to a surfaced drive, to reach North Lodge.

7 Go through the pedestrian gate at the lodge, then turn left and walk along the main drive for about 250yds (229m). Take the obvious footpath up the hillside on your left, between a short avenue of trees, to reach the top of the open, grassy ridge. Head for the hilltop folly, The Cage, then continue straight on to return to the house and car park.

WHILE YOU'RE THERE

The nearby Macclesfield Canal forms part of the Cheshire Ring Canal Walk, a 97-mile (156km) circular route around Greater Manchester incorporating the tow paths of six historic canals, including the Peak Forest and the Trent & Mersey. The stretch past Lyme Park, between Macclesfield and Marple, is rural and peaceful.

Chinley Churn and South Head

Two green hills rise above the Pennine village of Chinley on the edge of the Kinder moors.

DISTANCE 5 miles (8km)   MINIMUM TIME 3hrs

ASCENT/GRADIENT 950ft (290m) ▲▲▲ LEVEL OF DIFFICULTY ✚✚✚

PATHS Field paths, quarry and farm tracks, a few stiles

LANDSCAPE Hill pastures and moorland

SUGGESTED MAP OS Explorer OL1 Dark Peak

START / FINISH Grid reference: SK 041827

DOG FRIENDLINESS Dogs should be kept on lead

PARKING Village car park on Station Road

PUBLIC TOILETS None on route

Stand on the Hayfield to Chapel-en-le-Frith road at Chinley Head and you'll see two fine hills, South Head and Chinley Churn. Both are as green as the little combe of Otter Brook that separates them, and the field boundary walls that are emblazoned on their slopes like spider's webs only accentuate their graceful contours.

Victorian Monuments

The best base for exploring both of these hills is Chinley. Two sweeping curved viaducts that span the valley high above the town's rooftops are a reminder that this was once an important railway town: a junction for Sheffield, Manchester and Derby trains. The Rev'd Henry Thorald called the viaducts one of the greatest monuments to Victorian industrial England. At one time over 150 trains a day would have raced through the valley. At its height Chinley station had a café, a bookstall and bustling waiting rooms on every platform.

On leaving Chinley you are confronted by the rust-coloured crags, known as Cracken Edge. They form the upper of two distinct tiers. When you get closer the crags turn out to be the remains of old gritstone quarries. Further exploration reveals the entrances of shafts dug to extract the best stone; also part of the winding engine that conveyed the stone down to the valley below. Today the scene is one of degeneration, of rusty gears and grassy spoil heaps.

A Magnificent Panorama

When you reach the brow of the hill you're rewarded with a panorama of the second part of the walk. In it Kinder Scout peeps over the grassy peaks of Mount Famine and South Head. A pleasant grass track takes the route down from the edge back to the fields of Otter Brook's upper combe. At Chinley Head you come to a stark stone-built house with a strange name. Facing eastwards, the house catches the first of the morning sunshine that glints over the hilltops. That's why it's called Peep-O-Day. Note the small circular window built to catch those early rays of sunshine.

East of the Combe

The second part of the walk is spent on the eastern side of the combe of the Otter Brook. Another substantial old quarry track takes the route across the lower slopes of Mount Famine to a windswept little pass beneath South Head. From here the Sett Valley and the attractive field patterns surrounding South End farm are hidden by the gritstone rim of Mount Famine and the woods of Kinder Bank. The highland plateau of Kinder Scout has disappeared behind the spur of Kinderlow End. But it's only a matter of a short climb to the summit of South Head at 1,620ft (494m) to bring it all back in to view, and much more, before ending the day with an easy descent back into the valley below using farm tracks and field paths.

WALK 17

WALK 17 DIRECTIONS

❶ From the car park, turn left on Green Lane, then right up Maynestone Road to pass the war memorial. Leave the road for a signed path (grid ref 042828)

through a narrow ginnel on the left. Cross a stile, then climb north-west across fields towards Cracken Edge. At a cart track turn right, then left on a path passing between two hillside farmhouses. Go through a gate past the farm

WALK 17

on the right before climbing to the lower edge of the quarries.

2 Swing right on a sketchy path, passing a large hawthorn tree at the base of the grassy hillslope. You join a quarry track that zig-zags up the slope before heading northwards beneath quarry cliffs. Go over the stile in the fence across the track, then climb by this fence to the cliff top.

3 Turn right along a narrow edge path, then drop down to a wall-walked lower path past the quarried pits. Follow this over a stile and continue beneath the brow of the hill and past Whiterakes cottage.

4 Turn right on the track from Hills Farm and descend to a tarred lane which passes the evocatively named Peep-O-Day to the A624.

5 Cross over and turn left along the verge of the busy road. After 150yds (137m) an old cart track on the right goes past a small quarry. Turn right at a T-junction of tracks to follow the Pennine Bridleway across the lower, grassy slopes of Mount Famine.

6 It's worth making a detour to visit the top of South Head. Simply go through the gate by the National Trust sign and continue on the track to the summit. Resuming the main route, go right over a stile before the gate and descend south westwards to a walled track.

7 Follow this down to a crossroads of routes north of Andrews Farm. Go straight on into a field. The path soon develops into a track and joins the descending cart track from Andrews Farm.

8 On reaching the A624 turn right for 50yds (46m) and then cross to the signposted footpath, which cuts diagonally to the right corner of the first field before following a wall towards Otter Brook. As an old field boundary comes in from the right, the path turns half left to cross over the brook on a slabbed bridge.

9 A muddy path now climbs half left through scrubby woodland to reach Maynestone Road. Turn left and then follow the road back to Chinley war memorial.

A Walk to White Nancy Above Bollington

Exploring a short but scenic ridge, with a strange landmark, above the leafy town of Bollington.

DISTANCE *3.5 miles (5.7km)*   MINIMUM TIME *2hrs*

ASCENT/GRADIENT *1,180ft (360m)* ▲▲▲   LEVEL OF DIFFICULTY ✦✦✦

PATHS *Easy field paths and farm tracks, one short, sharp descent*

LANDSCAPE *Mostly gentle rolling pasture and small pockets of woodland*

SUGGESTED MAP *OS Explorer OL24 White Peak*

START / FINISH *Grid reference: SJ 937775*

DOG FRIENDLINESS *On lead through farmland, but off lead along lanes*

PARKING *Kerbside parking on Church Street or Lord Street, Bollington*

PUBLIC TOILETS *Bollington town centre*

Bollington lies just outside the far western edge of the Peak District National Park, but it continues to attract walkers and sightseers due in part to the short but inviting ridge of Kerridge Hill that overlooks the small Cheshire town. However it's not just the superb views that will hold your attention, but also the curiously shaped monument that occupies the far northern tip of the hill.

Striking Monument

Visible from below, and for some distance around for that matter since it stands at 920ft (280m) above sea level, White Nancy is a round stone construction that was built by the local Gaskell family in 1820 to commemorate the Battle of Waterloo. It was originally an open shelter with a stone table and benches, and was presumably a popular spot for picnics, but gradual decay and occasional vandalism led to it being bricked up, and now the building has no discernible door or windows. Nor does it bear any plaque or information panel, and most striking of all it is painted bright white. In terms of shape it resembles a large bell, or perhaps a giant chess pawn, with a large base that tapers into an odd little point. As for its name the most entertaining version suggests that Nancy was the name of one of the eight horses that pulled the heavy stone table to the summit when the tower was built. Beacons are still lit next to it to mark special occasions.

Stone Quarries

For all its scenic qualities the lower western slopes of Kerridge Hill are still quarried, although it's not visible on the walk until you reach the main summit ridge. The dressed stone is used for roofing slates and paving slabs and originally it was removed via narrow boats on the Macclesfield Canal that also served the mills and factories that once dotted the Bollington area. For a while shallow pits in the hill even yielded enough coal to supply the local engine houses, as steam power replaced water power during the Industrial Revolution's relentless advance. But inevitably your eye will be drawn to sights further afield, and if the weather is clear there will be good

BOLLINGTON

views across Macclesfield and the Cheshire Plain to the Mersey Estuary, the urban sprawl of Greater Manchester, as well as the long, high outline of the Pennines away to the north. Meanwhile White Nancy continues to sit impassively, a fittingly ambiguous monument to a past era when people felt compelled to mark the winning of a great overseas battle by building a picnic shelter on top of a small hill in Cheshire.

WALK 18 DIRECTIONS

❶ The walk starts towards the top of Lord Street (which Church Street leads into) where it turns sharply right at the top of a steep hill. Go along Cow Lane, a cul-de-sac, and through the gate at the far end. Take the upper of two field paths, heading half right across the sloping field on the right. Aim for

the gate and cattle grid at the far left top corner of the field.

❷ Turn left on to an open farm track and follow this all the way down to the lane in the bottom of the valley. Turn right, and fork right again past some terraced cottages on your right. A weir and pond below on your left are all that remain of the former silk

BOLLINGTON

mill. Follow this path through the Woodland Trust's cool and shady Waulkmill Wood.

❸ Leave the wood via a stile and go across the lower part of a sloping field, then in the second field aim for the buildings on the far side. Follow the gated path around to the right, and on through hillside fields.

❹ In the second field, fork left for the lower path that, beyond a gate, runs along the bottom edge of a new, mixed plantation, then down a walled track through woodland to reach the main road at Tower Hill.

❺ Turn right and walk along the pavement, past the Rising Sun Inn, for 0.5 mile (800m). Turn right into Lidgetts Lane, then as it bends almost immediately left go over a high stile ahead and on to a gated track past a row of

hawthorn trees. Swinging left follow this grassy path up to the ridge above – ignore the lower route by the right-hand fence.

❻ Follow the obvious hilltop track all the way along the spine of Kerridge Hill, ignoring tracks off left and right.

❼ After admiring the views at the monument (White Nancy) at the far end, drop sharply down the pitched path beyond, with Bollington spread out below, then cross a sunken farm lane and continue down across two more steep fields to reach a stile back into Cow Lane/Lord Street.

Overleaf: Combs Reservoir, Peak District National Park (Walk 19)

Combs Reservoir and Across Dickie's Meadow

A quiet corner of Derbyshire, between the Goyt and Chapel-en-le-Frith.

DISTANCE *3 miles (4.8km)*   MINIMUM TIME *2hrs 30min*

ASCENT/GRADIENT *164ft (50m)* ▲▲▲   LEVEL OF DIFFICULTY +++

PATHS *Can be muddy, quite a few stiles*

LANDSCAPE *Lakes, meadows, and high moors*

SUGGESTED MAP *OS Explorer OL24 White Peak*

START / FINISH *Grid reference: SK 033797*

DOG FRIENDLINESS *Farmland – dogs should be kept on leads*

PARKING *Combs reservoir car park*

PUBLIC TOILETS *None on route*

Combs lies in a quiet corner of north-west Derbyshire, off the road between Chapel-en-le-Frith and Whaley Bridge and beneath the sombre crag-fringed slopes of Combs Moss. This is a fine little corner of Derbyshire, tucked away from the crowds of Castleton and Hathersage.

Combs Reservoir

The route starts by the west side of the dam on a narrow path between the lake and Meveril Brook. Red campion, and thickets of dog rose line the path, which rounds the reservoir to its southern tip. You might see a pair of great crested grebes swimming among the rushes. Beyond the reservoir the path tucks under the railway, which brings to mind a mysterious story concerning Ned Dixon, who lived in nearby Tunstead Farm. Ned, or Dickie as he was known, was brutally murdered by his cousin. Locals say his spirit lived on in his skull, which was left outside to guard against intruders. Strange things were said to happen when anybody tried to remove the skull. It is also claimed that the present road from Combs to Chapel was constructed because the railway bridge would not stand over Dane Hey Road. After the first bridge was completed it collapsed, burying the workmen's tools. This was blamed on the skull: Dickie had been against the railway going across Tunstead land.

Combs

A lane with hedges of honeysuckle and hawthorn winds into the village of Combs, where a handful of stone-built cottages are centred on the welcoming Beehive Inn. Combs' most famous son is Herbert Froode. He made his name in automotive engineering as one of the inventors of the brake lining. Starting out in the early 1890s he developed woven cotton brakes for horse-drawn wagons, but his ideas didn't really take off until 1897 when the first motor buses emerged. Froode applied his knowledge of brakes to this much greater challenge and by the end of the century had won a contract to supply brake linings for the new London omnibuses. Ferodo, his company, is an anagram of his surname.

COMBS RESERVOIR

Final Views

Through the village the route takes to the hillsides. Now Combs Reservoir, which is spread beneath your feet, looks every bit a natural lake. Beyond it are the plains of Manchester and the hazy blue West Pennine horizon. In the other direction the gritstone cliffs of Combs Edge, which look rather like those of Kinder Scout, overshadow the sullen combe of Pyegreave Brook.

This very pleasing walk ends as it starts, by the shores of the reservoir. If you look along the line of the dam towards the right of two farms, you'll see where Dickie lived. He's probably watching you, too.

WALK 19 DIRECTIONS

1 Follow the path from the dam along the reservoir's western shore, ignoring the first footbridge over Meveril Brook.

2 As the reservoir narrows the path traverses small fields, then comes to another footbridge over the brook. This time cross it and head south across another field. Beyond a foot tunnel under the

73

Buxton line railway, the path reaches a narrow hedge-lined country lane. Turn left along the lane into Combs village.

❸ Past the Beehive Inn in the village centre, take the lane straight ahead, then the left fork, signposted to Dove Holes. This climbs out of the village towards Combs Edge.

WHERE TO EAT AND DRINK

The Beehive Inn at Combs is a splendid little pub serving fine bar meals. Alternatively, there's the more formal Hanging Gate Inn at Cockyard.

❹ Take the second footpath on the left, which begins at a muddy clearing just beyond Millway Cottage. Go through the stile and climb on a partially slabbed path and then uphill across pasture with the wall on your right. Away to the right is the huge comb of Pygreave Brook. Climb the pathless spur and go through gateways in the next two boundary walls before following a wall on the right. Ignore a gate in this wall – that's a path to Bank Hall Farm – but stay with the narrow path raking across rough grassy hillslopes with the railway line and the reservoir below left.

❺ The path comes down to a track that runs alongside the railway line. This joins a lane just short of the Lodge. Turn left to go under the railway and north to Down Lee Farm.

WHILE YOU'RE THERE

Take a look around charming Chapel-en-le-Frith, a traditional market town with a cobbled square and the 14th-century Church of St Thomas à Becket. In 1648 1,500 Scottish soldiers were taken prisoner and locked in the church after the Battle of Ribbleton Moor. Forty-eight soldiers died in what was to be known as the Black Hole of Derbyshire.

❻ Turn left through a kissing gate 200yds (183m) beyond the farmhouse. The signposted path follows an overgrown hedge towards Marsh Hall Farm. The fields can become very boggy on the final approaches. When you reach the farm complex turn right over a stile and follow a vehicle track heading north-west.

❼ After 200yds (183m) turn left on a field path that heads west to a stile at the edge of the Chapel-en-le-Frith golf course. Waymarking arrows show the way across the fairway. The stile marking the exit from the golf course is 300yds (274m) short of the clubhouse. You then cross a small field to reach the B5470.

❽ Turn left along the road (there's a pavement on the far side), and follow it past the Hanging Gate pub at Cockyard. After passing the entrance to the sailing club, turn left to cross over the dam of Combs Reservoir and return to the car park.

WHAT TO LOOK OUT FOR

On a winter's day in 1995 a group of birders saw something they hadn't been expecting. While wandering by the west shores they came across some huge clawed footprints sunk deep into the mud. After studying the photographs they had taken it became obvious that a huge cat had been on the prowl – probably the Peak Panther that has had many sightings locally.

The Moorland Ramparts of Carl Wark

Tramp along medieval packhorse trails in search of the dwelling place of ancient Britons.

DISTANCE 5.5 miles (8.8km)   MINIMUM TIME 3hrs
ASCENT/GRADIENT 328ft (100m) ▲▲▲ LEVEL OF DIFFICULTY +++
PATHS Generally good paths
LANDSCAPE Millstone tors and quarries, heather moors and woodland
SUGGESTED MAP OS Explorer OL1 Dark Peak
START / FINISH Grid reference: SK 252801
DOG FRIENDLINESS Keep on lead near sheep, particularly at lambing time
PARKING Surprise View pay car park on A6187 east of Hathersage
PUBLIC TOILETS None on route

On the moors beyond Hathersage, history and geology combine to produce a fascinating panorama. The main stone bed from which this area is formed is Chatsworth grit, a coarse, gritty, sandstone, with scattered pebbles, that is extremely resistant to erosion. This was once much valued as a building material and many Peak District buildings, including Chatsworth House, are constructed from it.

The other major use to which it was put was to fashion grinding stones for the emerging Sheffield tool and cutlery industry and to provide millstones for grinding corn. Millstone Edge was once a thriving quarrying area. However the introduction of carborundum (a synthetic abrasive) in the 20th century led to a fall in demand for millstone grit and the consequent demise of the quarrying industry. The quarrymen may have gone but they have left piles of half-fashioned millstones lying amidst the debris of quarried stone near the start of this walk.

Burbage Edge

The escarpment that forms Burbage Edge is an impressive backdrop for a series of flat-topped hills rising from the moor. Over Owler Tor, Winyards Nick, Higger Tor and Carl Wark were once part of the same sandstone bed as Burbage Edge but were displaced by faulting. With their concave sides, bare gritstone edges and level surfaces these uplands were ideal sites for fortification. There are at least nine fine examples of hill-forts in the Peak District probably dating from the Iron Age, and Carl Wark is certainly one of the most spectacular. It is lower in height than its neighbour, Higger Tor, but it is defended naturally on all but one of its sides by very steep slopes. On the undefended side a stone rampart has been built, about 20ft (6m) wide at the base with boulders bonded to a wall of turf. In the south-west corner, where the defensive wall turns inwards, lies what would once have been the entrance to the fort.

The age of the fort has never been satisfactorily settled. One school of thought would place it in the post-Roman period of the 5th and 6th centuries AD because of the technique used in building the stone and turf

CARL WARK

wall, and because of similarities with the construction of Dark Age (AD 500–1100) forts in Scotland. Others have argued that the 'in-turned' entrance suggests a much earlier Iron Age construction. Gardom's Edge, near Baslow to the south, which is very similar to Carl Wark in that its interior is small and rocky with little space for buildings, is actually a neolithic enclosure, however nothing has yet been found at Carl Wark to date it from this time. The controversy will continue but probably Carl Wark was originally an Iron or Bronze Age construction, which was re-fortified at the end of the Roman occupation.

WALK 20 DIRECTIONS

❶ From the car park at Surprise View go through a kissing gate and uphill on a well-worn path. At a large group of stones the path veers left and continues uphill towards Over Owler Tor. Just before this go left on a smaller track, head downhill and towards a fence. Turn right at the fence.

❷ Continue following this track until it meets with a dry-stone wall that has been running parallel with the track. Follow the path right from here past the end of a large sheepfold. Continue walking ahead on the moorland path. The rocky outcrop of Higger Tor is now on the left and Carl Wark is ahead to the right.

3 When the path forks, veer right. Continue past Carl Wark, keeping it to the right. Go downhill towards the far right corner of a wood. Cross over a stone bridge then a wooden bridge, head uphill on a well-worn path to join an old green road and then turn left.

4 Continue along this track with Burbage Rocks above you and to the right. At Upper Burbage Bridge cross two streams via large

stones, head uphill and follow the upper of two paths to the left and uphill. Continue across open moorland then ascend Higger Tor on a stone stepped path. Cross the tor then descend the other side near the south-east corner.

5 Follow the track across the moor towards Carl Wark. Ascend this and turn left to reach the summit. After looking around at the views return to the top of the path and, keeping the stone ramparts on your left, descend via a path southwards.

6 From here the path heads across a boggy section of moor, curves round a small, rocky hill then heads downhill towards the A6187. Cross on to this road via a stile, cross the road and turn right on to a pavement.

7 Turn left through a gate and down to a footbridge. Turn right on to the Waterside path.

8 At the next footbridge, turn right for the wide, sunken path between the heather. At the top, cross the road for the car park.

On the Edge at Stanage

Skirting the gritstone cliffs which line Sheffield's moorland edge.

DISTANCE 9 miles (14.5km)	**MINIMUM TIME** 5hrs
ASCENT/GRADIENT 1,150ft (350m) ▲▲▲	**LEVEL OF DIFFICULTY** +++

PATHS Well-defined paths and tracks, a few stiles

LANDSCAPE Gritstone and heather moorland

SUGGESTED MAP OS Explorer OL1 Dark Peak

START / FINISH Grid reference: SK 232814

DOG FRIENDLINESS Dogs are banned from north-western part of Stanage Edge due to nesting birds; elsewhere keep on lead

PARKING Pay car park, Oddfellows Road, Hathersage

PUBLIC TOILETS Main road, Hathersage, and on lane above North Lees

From Moscar to Baslow a line of dark cliffs cap the heather moors east of the Derwent Valley. Defoe, ever the scourge of mountain scenery, called it a vast extended moor or waste in which strangers would be obliged to take guides or lose their way. Later Emily Brontë came here to visit her friend Ellen Nussey, the wife of the local vicar. Emily would have found the place much more acceptable, and not unlike her home at Haworth.

Early Climbers

In the 1890s, the climber, JW Putrell turned to the highest of these cliffs, Stanage Edge, and pioneered several gully routes. Others would follow and today Stanage and its neighbouring 'edges' are one of the most popular climbing venues in Britain. But Stanage is a great place for walkers too, for they can stride out on firm skyline paths with Yorkshire on one side and Derbyshire on the other. High car parks mean that you can walk Stanage without much ascent, but it's more rewarding to work for your fun, so we'll start the route at Hathersage.

The Eyres of Hathersage

Hathersage is a neat village by the banks of the River Derwent. The route starts gently on Baulk Lane and passes the cricket ground on its way through the little valley of Hood Brook. Gradients steepen and the route comes across the 16th-century castellated manor of North Lees Hall, the inspiration for Thornfield Hall, Mr Rochester's home in Jane Eyre. The Eyre family did exist in real life. They were Roman Catholics who lived in the hall until the 17th century, when a narrow-minded Protestant community drove them out. The remains of a chapel, built in 1685, only to be destroyed three years later, can still be seen in the grounds.

Above the hall the route climbs on to the moors and a paved causey track known as Jacob's Ladder takes it to the top of the cliffs. The cliff-edge path to High Neb and Crow Chin is a delight, and the views from it are extensive, taking in a good deal of the Derwent and Hope valleys, Mam Tor and Kinder Scout. It may seem strange to descend to the foot of the cliffs, but the lost height doesn't amount to much and you can now view them from the perspective of the climber.

HATHERSAGE

After rejoining the edge, the path passes above Robin Hood's Cave, where the legendary outlaw perhaps hid from the Sheriff of Nottingham, to reach the high road and climbers' car park. Now there's just Higger Tor to do. The rocky knoll surrounded by an ocean of heather makes a fine finale, one last lofty perch before the descent back to Hathersage.

WALK 21 DIRECTIONS

❶ At the car park in Hathersage, take the path in the corner past the Methodist church to Main Road. Turn right, cross over, then turn left in Baulk Lane. The lane climbs steadily north, passing the cricket ground. Beyond the buildings it becomes an unsurfaced track.

❷ Just short of Cowclose Farm take the signposted left fork, which passes to the right of Brookfield Manor to reach a country lane. Turn right here, then left along a drive to North Lees Hall. After rounding the hall, turn right, climbing some steps that cut the corner to another track. This crosses hillside pastures before continuing through woodland.

79

3 A stepped path on the left makes a short cut to a roadside toilet block and mountain rescue post. Cross the road for a grassy path heading for the rocks of Stanage Edge. After 200yds (183m) you join the path from the nearby car park. A paved path now climbs through Stanage Plantation before arcing left to the cliff top and turning left.

4 Follow the firm edge-top path north-westwards to see the impressive summit of High Neb and Crow Chin.

5 When you reach Crow Chin, where the edge veers north, descend to a lower path that doubles back beneath the cliffs. This eventually joins a track from the right, which returns the route to the top of the cliffs. Continue walking towards the south-east along the edge to the bouldery east summit (marked on Ordnance Survey maps by a spot height of 457m), whose rocks are capped by a concrete trig point.

WHERE TO EAT AND DRINK

The Scotsman's Pack, on School Lane, Hathersage, is an old coaching inn serving Burtonwood beers and excellent bar meals. It has outside seating by a tinkling stream. There's often a snack van on the car park at Upper Burbage Bridge.

6 The track continues to the road at Upper Burbage Bridge. Proceed left along the road for about 150yds (137m), then turn right by the car park, taking the the higher of the two paths which head south to the lofty heights of the summit of Higger Tor.

7 From the rocky top, double back (roughly north of north-

WHAT TO LOOK FOR

Beneath the cliffs of Stanage Edge you'll see piles of old millstones and grindstones, some intact, and some incomplete. They are the abandoned relics of an industry that supplied the flourishing steelworks of Sheffield and local corn mills. French imports, which were both cheaper and better, and the coming of the roller mills saw the decline of the industry by the 1860s.

west) on a path to the Fiddler's Elbow road. Slightly uphill along the road take the path on the left. This descends Callow Bank to reach a walled track leading down to the Dale Bottom road. Follow the road for 300yds (274m) to a track on the right that traverses the hillslopes to Toothill Farm. Turn left by the farmhouse on a drive that soon joins a tarred lane taking the route down to Hathersage's impressively spired church and the Roman fort of Camp Green.

8 Turn right down School Lane to reach Main Road, which leads you back into the centre of Hathersage. Go left before the toilets to reach the car park.

WHILE YOU'RE THERE

Take a look round the parish Church of St Michael, which you pass on the hillsides above the village. It dates back to the 14th century, though the Perpendicular tower and its spire are 100 years younger. The stained-glass east window comes from the doomed church of Derwent before it was submerged beneath the rising waters of Ladybower Reservoir. In the churchyard a particularly long grave is claimed to be that of Robin Hood's henchman, Little John.

Sacred Worship on Stanton Moor

A short circular walk across the mysterious Stanton Moor to discover the goings-on of ancient Druids and devilish dancers.

DISTANCE 4 miles (6.4km) **MINIMUM TIME** 3hrs

ASCENT/GRADIENT 540ft (165m) ▲▲▲ **LEVEL OF DIFFICULTY** +++

PATHS Firm moorland tracks and field paths, a few stiles

LANDSCAPE Heather moorland and rolling pastoral landscapes

SUGGESTED MAP OS Explorer OL24 White Peak

START / FINISH Grid reference: SJ 938697

DOG FRIENDLINESS On lead around livestock

PARKING Roadside parking on Main Street, Birchover

PUBLIC TOILETS Main Street, Birchover

Stanton Moor is a small and distinctive upthrust of gritstone amid the limestone dales of the White Peak. It's moorland in miniature, where heather and silver birch provides a marked contrast to the rolling pasture and undulating river valleys all around. To the east it looks down on to the Derwent Valley and Matlock, while to the west there are panoramic views across to Bakewell and the valley of the River Wye.

Dancing on the Sabbath

There has been human activity on Stanton Moor for thousands of years. The whole of the moor is a Scheduled Ancient Monument, dotted with dozens of ancient cairns, barrows and tumuli, although much of it is hidden by heather, gorse and bilberry. Since the Bronze Age, settlers have favoured the moor for the protection that this high vantage point must have offered. However, it's association with Druids and ritual worship that has made Stanton Moor particularly well known. Nine Ladies stone circle, situated in a clearing in the silver birch, has nine stones, which are supposed to represent women that were caught dancing on the Sabbath and turned to stone. The King Stone, set back from the circle, is the unfortunate fiddler.

Antiquarians over the centuries have made much of Stanton Moor as a magnet for Druidical activity, with the bizarre rock carvings at Rowtor Rocks interpreted as sacrificial basins, altars and rock cells for some ungodly practice. Although there's little evidence of ritual worship and human sacrifice ever having taken place, the moor exudes an air of mystery that makes it a great place to explore. And if you visit during the summer solstice you will be treated to the sight of hundreds of Pagan revellers, travellers and hippies celebrating around Nine Ladies – so perhaps the Druids' tradition lives on.

Gritstone blocks and towers

On the route across the moor you will pass several giant blocks of gritstone standing isolated among the heather. Each has its own name – the Cork Stone, Heart Stone, Twopenny Loaf and the Cat Stone. They are all natural lumps of stone, weathered into fantastic shapes. Some believe that they were once probably objects of Pagan worship, although now their devotees are usually climbers who use them for practice or 'bouldering'.

As you walk along the eastern edge of the moor you'll pass what's known as the Earl Grey Tower. This folly was built by the Thornhill family, whose descendants still live at nearby Stanton Hall, to celebrate the passing of Grey's historic Reform Bill in 1832 which gave men the vote. The square stone tower (National Trust) is no longer open due to safety reasons.

WALK 22 DIRECTIONS

1 From the Druid Inn at the end of Main Street take the signposted footpath on the bend opposite. Follow this up along a wooded ridge above the village. Where it ends at a quarry car park go left on to the road. After 0.25 miles (400m) turn right for a signposted path on to the moor.

2 Go over a stile and veer left at the Cork Stone for a wide path across the middle of the heather moor. Stay on the main path as it enters silver birch scrub, then swing right on a wide grassy track, with a fence over to the left, until you reach Nine Ladies.

3 At Nine Ladies, walk to the interpretation panel and turn left on the main path. In 50 yds (46m) fork right for a path through the gorse and heather. Go over a stile and turn right on to a path along the high wooded edge of the moor to Earl Grey Tower. Continue on this now open path until you reach a stile in the fence on your right.

4 Cross over the stile and at the junction of tracks turn left. At a crossroads of routes turn left again, downhill, to reach the road. Turn right and walk along this for 50yds (46m) and go left on a footpath.

5 Follow this well-signposted route along the left-hand edge of a camping field, and then around some buildings and ahead on a rough farm track along the right-hand edge of two successive fields. When you meet the unsurfaced Clough Lane turn right.

6 Walk along the lane to its end, at Cowley Knoll Farm. Turn left on to a surfaced lane and almost immediately turn right, by Uppertown Farm, for a gated path through fields. After hugging a wall on the right the

path continues past a cottage and begins a huge loop around the hilly outcrop of Bradley Rocks. At the far end go through a gate to reach a path junction.

7 Unless you are extending the walk to visit Robin Hood's Stride, ignore the path downhill to the left and continue with the level track as it swings back east towards Birchover. Joining a gravel drive on a bend, take the lower route and at a crossroads of lanes go straight on past the church to return to Birchover village and Main Street. If you want to explore Rowtor Rocks look for the narrow path on the left just before the Druid Inn.

EXTENDING THE WALK

You can extend this walk at **7** to visit Robin Hood's Stride and the Hermit's Cave. Follow the path steeply down to the road in the valley bottom, turn left and cross over for the path up to the rocks. Return the same way.

WALK 23

The Goyt Valley of the Grimshawes

A Manchester family's country retreat gave way to the demand for water.

DISTANCE *3.5 miles (5.7km)*   **MINIMUM TIME** *2hrs 30min*

ASCENT/GRADIENT *984ft (300m)* ▲▲▲   **LEVEL OF DIFFICULTY** ✦✦✦

PATHS *Good paths and tracks, a few stiles*

LANDSCAPE *Park type woodland and moor*

SUGGESTED MAP *OS Explorer OL24 White Peak*

START / FINISH *Grid reference: SK 012748*

DOG FRIENDLINESS *Dogs should be kept under close control*

PARKING *Errwood car park*

PUBLIC TOILETS *I mile (1.6km) south at Derbyshire Bridge car park*

The River Goyt begins its journey on the moors of Axe Edge and Goyt Moss before flowing northwards to join the Mersey at Stockport. In times past its remote upper valley would have been filled with oakwoods. An old salters' and smugglers' road known as the Street, straddled it at Goyt Bridge before climbing over the Shining Tor ridge at Pym Chair.

Errwood Hall

In 1830, the Manchester industrialist Samuel Grimshawe chose this remote valley to build Errwood Hall, as a wedding present for his son. The family lived here 'in the style of princes'. They imported 40,000 rhododendrons and azaleas for the ornate gardens, using their own ocean yacht, the *Mariquita*. In its heyday the estate had a staff of 20, and included a coal mine, a watermill, housing for the servants and a private school.

The Building of the Reservoirs

But even the Grimshawes and all their accumulated wealth couldn't resist Stockport's ever-growing need for water, and in 1938 the house was demolished for the newly built Fernilee Reservoir. The dark battalions of spruce and larch, planted for a quick and plentiful supply of timber, eventually engulfed the oakwoods, and 30 years later a second reservoir, the Errwood, was built, higher up the valley. Little Goyt Bridge was dismantled and rebuilt upstream; and the valley was changed forever. For a while it became the destination of seemingly every Sunday car outing from Greater Manchester. The valley's single road was choked by vehicles and that remoteness and quiet seemed lost forever. Then a pioneering traffic management scheme was initiated by the National Park authority, including new car parks, a bus service and even road closures. The result was that this once peaceful beauty spot was restored to a state of relative tranquillity.

Back to the Grimshawes

This walk takes you back to the 19th century, to the time of the Grimshawes, but first you aim to get an overview of the valley by climbing the grassy spur dividing the Goyt and Shooter's Clough. After dropping into Shooter's Clough the path wanders through unruly streamside woodland to green pastures and a wooded knoll. You briefly rejoin the crowds on the way to Errwood Hall. As you pass through mossy gateposts and into the grounds the order of the garden has been ruffled by nature, but the rhododendrons still bloom bright in the summer. The mossy foundations and floors still exist, as do some of the lower walls, arched windows and doors. You leave the hall and the crowds behind to round a wooded hill.

The Spanish Shrine

Uphill in a wild, partially wooded comb lies the Spanish Shrine, built by the Grimshawes in memory of their governess, Dolores de Bergrin. Inside the circular stone-built shrine there's a fine altar and colourful mosaic. If the weather is clement your spirits will be lifted by the return walk along the crest of Foxlow Edge, for you can see most of today's walk laid beneath your feet as you survey the wild rolling moors, which are dappled with heather, bracken and pale moor grasses. Dinghies may be racing across the waters of Errwood Reservoir and even the intrusive sprucewoods seem to fit this exquisite jigsaw.

WALK 23 DIRECTIONS

1 The path, signposted to Stakeside and Cat and Fiddle, begins from the roadside just south of the car park. Climb with it through a copse of trees, go straight across a cart track, then climb the grassy spur separating Shooter's Clough and the Goyt Valley.

2 Go through a gate in the wall that runs along the spur and then follow a path that zig-zags through the woodland of Shooter's Clough before fording a stream. The path heads north (right), through rhododendron bushes before continuing across open grassland fields to a signposted junction of footpaths.

3 Turn right here on a track skirting the near side of a wooded knoll, then ignoring the first path through gateposts, take the second left 'to 'Errwood Hall'. The path continues past the ruins, before descending some steps to cross a stream via footbridge.

4 Climb some steps on the right to reach another footpath signpost. Turn left along the path signposted 'The Shrine and Pym Chair'. This gradually swings north on hillslopes beneath Foxlow Edge. There's a short detour down and left to see the Spanish Shrine (visible from the main path).

5 About 100yds (91m) on from the shrine the path reaches open moorland. Take the path forking right, which climbs to the top of Foxlow Edge. On reaching some old quarry workings near the top, the path is joined by a tumbledown dry-stone wall. Keep to the left-hand side of the wall, except for one short stretch where the path goes the other side to avoid some crosswalls.

WHAT TO LOOK OUT FOR

On the west slopes of Burbage Edge you'll see the old trackbed of the Cromford and High Peak Railway, from the tunnel near the top down to the shores of Errwood Reservoir. Although this famous railway was one of the earliest in the country, the branch through the Goyt Valley was only in use between 1852 and 1877.

Ignore any paths off left or right and stay with the ridge route. A wall (right) and a fence (left) soon confine the path as it descends to the woods.

6 At a fence corner, by the woodland's edge, follow the path left, downhill through the trees where it's joined by another path. With banks of rhododendron bushes on your right, descend to the roadside at Shooter's Clough Bridge just 100yds (91m) north of the car park.

EXTENDING THE WALK

You can make a satisfying upland extension to this walk by ascending by the side of Shooter's Clough from Point **2**. Join the moorland ridge over Shining Tor and Cats Tor to join the road at Pym Chair. Turn right, down The Street and rejoin the main route near Point **5**.

Ghosts of Miller's Dale

The rural serenity of modern Miller's Dale belies its early role in the Industrial Revolution.

DISTANCE 6 miles (9.7km)   **MINIMUM TIME** 3hrs 30min

ASCENT/GRADIENT 690ft (210m) ▲▲▲   **LEVEL OF DIFFICULTY** +++

PATHS Generally well-defined paths and tracks, path in Water-cum-Jolly Dale liable to flooding, quite a few stiles

LANDSCAPE Limestone dales

SUGGESTED MAP OS Explorer OL24 White Peak

START / FINISH Grid reference: SK 154743

DOG FRIENDLINESS Dogs can run free in dales with no livestock, but keep under control when crossing farmland

PARKING Tideswell Dale pay car park

PUBLIC TOILETS At car park

It's all quiet in Miller's Dale these days, but it wasn't always so. Many early industrialists wanted to build their cotton mills in the countryside, far away from the marauding Luddites of the city. The Wye and its tributaries had the power to work these mills. The railway followed, and that brought more industry with it. And so little Miller's Dale and its neighbours joined the Industrial Revolution.

The walk starts in Tideswell Dale. Nowadays it's choked with thickets and herbs but they hide a history of quarrying and mining for basalt.

Cruelty at the Mill

Litton Mill will eventually be modernised into holiday cottages, but today it lies damp and derelict in a shadowy part of the dale. *The Memoirs of Robert Blincoe*, written in 1863, tells of mill owner Ellis Needham's cruelty to child apprentices, who were often shipped in from the poorhouses of London. Many of the children died and were buried in the churchyards of Tideswell and Taddington. It is said that ghosts of some of the apprentices still make appearances in or around the mill. The walk emerges from the shadows of the mill into Water-cum-Jolly Dale. At first the river is lined by mudbanks thick with rushes and common horsetail. It's popular with wildfowl. The river widens out and, at the same time, impressive limestone cliffs squeeze the path. The river's widening is artificial, a result of it being controlled to form a head of water for the downstream mill.

Round the next corner is Cressbrook Mill, built by Sir Richard Arkwright, but taken over by William Newton. Newton also employed child labour but was said to have treated them well. The rooftop bell tower would have peeled to beckon the apprentices, who lived next door, to the works. Like Litton this impressive Georgian mill was allowed to moulder, but is now being restored as flats. The walk leaves the banks of the Wye at Cressbrook to take in pretty Cressbrook Dale. In this nature reserve you'll see lily-of-the-valley, wild garlic and bloody cranesbill; you should also see bee and fragrant orchids. Just as you think you've found your true rural retreat you'll climb to the rim of the dale, look across it and see the grassed-over spoil heaps of lead mines. Finally, the ancient strip fields of Litton form a mosaic of pasture and dry-stone walls on the return route.

WALK 24 DIRECTIONS

❶ Follow the path southwards from beside the car park toilet block into Tideswell Dale, taking the right-hand fork to cross over the little bridge.

❷ On entering Miller's Dale, go left along the tarmac lane

to Litton Mill. Go through the gateposts on to a concessionary path through a mill yard. Beyond the mill, the path follows the River Wye, as it meanders through the tight, steep-sided dale.

❸ The river widens out in Water-cum-Jolly Dale and the path, which is liable to flooding here, traces a wall of limestone cliffs before reaching Cressbrook. Cross the footbridge and then turn left to pass in front of Cressbrook Mill and out on to the road.

4 Turn left along the road and then take the right fork which climbs steadily into Cressbrook Dale. Where the road doubles back uphill, leave it for a track going straight ahead into the woods. The track degenerates into a narrow path that emerges in a clearing high above the stream. Follow it downhill to a footbridge over the stream and then take the right fork path, which climbs high up the valley side to a stile in the top wall.

5 Do not cross the stile, instead take the downhill path to reach the dale bottom, where there's a junction of paths. The one that's wanted here recrosses the stream on stepping stones, and then climbs into Tansley Dale.

6 The path turns right at the top of the dale, follows a tumbledown wall before crossing it on a step stile. Head for a wall corner in the next field, then onwards through a narrow enclosure to reach a walled track just south of Litton village.

7 Turn left along the track, which comes out on to a country lane at the crown of a sharp bend. Keep straight on down the lane

but leave it at the next bend for a cross-field path to Bottomhill Road. Across the road, a further field path descends to the lane at Dale House Farm. Turn left and then right on a lane marked 'unsuitable for motors'. Follow this road into Tideswell.

8 After looking around the village head south down the main street, then right on to Gordon Road, which then heads south.

9 Where this ends, continue down the stony track ahead, which runs parallel with the main road. At the end go through a small gate on the left fork, down to the road into Tideswell Dale. Cross over and turn right for a short path, back to the car park.

EXTENDING THE WALK

If it's dry you can extend this walk though Monk's Dale. Leave the main route at Point **8** in Tideswell and rejoin it from the Monsal Trail, back at Litton Mill, near Point **2**, to retrace your steps to the start of the walk.

Hunt for Wild Boar in Macclesfield Forest

A circular walk exploring the old and new Macclesfield Forest, and the mini Matterhorn of Shutlingsloe.

> **DISTANCE** 7 miles (11.3km) **MINIMUM TIME** 3hrs 30min
>
> **ASCENT/GRADIENT** 2,820ft (860m) ▲▲▲ **LEVEL OF DIFFICULTY** +++
>
> **PATHS** Sloping field paths, lanes and easy forest tracks, steep hillside, lots of stiles
>
> **LANDSCAPE** Rough pasture, angular hills, plus large tracts of woodland
>
> **SUGGESTED MAP** OS Explorer OL24 White Peak
>
> **START / FINISH** Grid reference: SJ 980681
>
> **DOG FRIENDLINESS** On lead in fields, off lead on lanes and in woodland, unless notices indicate otherwise
>
> **PARKING** Lay-by at Brookside, on lane 0.75 mile (1.2km) south of Wildboarclough
>
> **PUBLIC TOILETS** At Macclesfield Forest Visitor Centre

The Royal Forest of Macclesfield was once the preserve of the nobility, an extensive hunting ground for the royal court where the likes of deer and boar were keenly sought out. It covered a large area, stretching across from the Cheshire Plain to the valleys of the Goyt and Dane; but most of the so-called 'forest' was probably little more than open ground or scrub, with large tracts of high and inhospitable moorland.

In the 1400s Henry VI appointed John Stanley as Steward of Macclesfield Forest, and it was his son Thomas (later Baron Stanley) who played a crucial role in the Battle of Bosworth in 1485 to ensure the victory of his stepson – the Earl of Richmond, who became Henry VII. The grateful new king made Stanley the Earl of Derby, and the office of Steward of Macclesfield Forest became a hereditary position.

Tough Forest Laws

The Forest Laws that operated in the hunting lands until Elizabethan times were extremely strict. There were severe penalties for anyone caught poaching, as testified by the name of the isolated hilltop pub that the walk visits at Higher Sutton. It's located at a point where a route left the original forest boundary and poachers caught in the act could expect a bleak outcome – the pub is called the Hanging Gate. Other rights in the forest were jealously guarded and fines and punishments were available to reprimand locals who took firewood or let their stock wander. Near the start of the walk is the equally descriptive Crag Inn, tucked away above Clough Brook at Wildboarclough. But whether, according to local tradition, 'the ravine of the wild boar' is indeed the location of the last of its kind killed in England during the 15th century is open to doubt.

Looming above Wildboarclough is the coned peak of Shutlingsloe, which at 1,659ft (506m) offers a full 360-degree panoramic view over Cheshire, Staffordshire and Derbyshire. Especially prominent is Tegg's Nose, a gritstone outcrop to the north that protrudes above the dark green conifers of the present-day Macclesfield Forest. This modern plantation produces timber

MACCLESFIELD FOREST

rather than venison, although native broadleaved trees such as rowan, oak and silver birch have been planted in recent years to break up the regimented rows of spruces and larches and provide encouragement for wildlife. Walkers are welcome to explore the forest's many paths and tracks that climb the often steep hillsides. Look out for the occasional wooden sculpture, and wildlife such as crossbills and woodpeckers, stoats and foxes. The heronry in the larch trees on the eastern shore of Trentabank Reservoir is the largest in the Peak District. In addition, the forest does apparently have red deer, but you'll have to be very quiet and patient to catch a glimpse.

WALK 25 DIRECTIONS

❶ Walk along the road for 440yds (402m) to the Crag Inn, then at the foot of its drive go over a stile on the left for a path across a sloping field. This maintains its direction through successive fields

(each with a wall gate) until finally you reach the tarmac farm drive at the very top. Turn left and walk along this drive to the lane.

❷ Turn right at the far end and walk along the lane as far as Greenway Bridge. Go over a stile on the right and follow the path beside the stream, until it crosses it in order to veer left, up Oakenclough. Keep to the bottom of this little valley, past a ruined stone shelter, and as it rises continue to its far head, near a small pond. Turn right on to a private drive and then go almost immediately left for a wall-side path uphill.

3 At the top go over a stile and strike out across moorland on a clear grassy track. Maintain your direction until you reach a stile on the far side. Go over this and then descend on a sunken, fenced track to emerge opposite the Hanging Gate pub.

4 Turn right and follow the road for a mile (1.6km), keeping straight on at the junction where the road bends sharply left. Ignore another turning on the left, until finally the lane turns right, into Macclesfield Forest, where there's a wide gate on the right.

5 Don't go through the main gate. Instead go over the stile to the left, signposted 'Shutlingsloe/ Trentabank', and follow the footpath which runs parallel with the lane. After dropping down to a newly planted area, cross the

footbridge and at the junction of tracks near the wood sculpture carry straight on up a wide, stony route. At the far end turn right, or for the visitor centre and toilets at Trentabank turn left.

6 Walk up the wide forest drive and go left at a fork, then at the far end turn right for a long but quite easy gravel track up through the trees. At the top go through a gate and continue straight on, then turn right to leave the forest for a stone-flagged path across the open moorland up towards the distinctive top of Shutlingsloe.

7 From the summit descend the eroded track down the steep eastern slope of the hill, until you eventually turn right on to an open farm drive. Follow this all the way down to the road and turn right to the car park.

Right: River near Wildboarclough, Peak District National Park (Walk 25)

From Dark to White

On conical Chrome Hill the dramatic landscape changes, from limestone to gritstone.

DISTANCE 7.5 miles (12.1km) **MINIMUM TIME** 4hrs 30min

ASCENT/GRADIENT 980ft (300m) ▲▲▲ **LEVEL OF DIFFICULTY** +++

PATHS Good paths except for ones between Hollinsclough and Brand End, can be slippery after rain, lots of stiles

LANDSCAPE Gritstone moors and cloughs with limestone hills

SUGGESTED MAP OS Explorer OL24 White Peak

START / FINISH Grid reference: SK 034697

DOG FRIENDLINESS Farmland, dogs should be kept under close control

PARKING Axe Edge car park

PUBLIC TOILETS None on route

When you stand on Axe Edge, you're standing on the Pennine watershed. Just to prove it, five rivers, the Goyt, the Dane, the Dove, the Wye and the Manifold, go their separate ways towards the Irish and North seas from near here. You're 1,660ft (506m) above sea level on one of the wildest gritstone moors of the Dark Peak, but when you look east you're looking across to the White Peak valley of the Dove. It's a fascinating view with several rocky hills vying for attention. One angular one stands out from all the rest – that's Chrome Hill, and it's the highpoint of the day.

A narrow lane takes the walk down into the valley, and soon you're following an old green road beneath Leap Edge. If you can hear buzzing noises it's not your ears: it's either that of racing cars on the nearby High Edge Raceway or model aeroplanes soaring on the thermals of the hillside.

The Dragon's Back

Chrome Hill hides behind Hollins Hill for a while, but once you've climbed round the limestone knoll of Tor Rock you see it again rearing up into the sky. It's hard to believe, but Chrome Hill and its neighbours are the remains of coral reefs formed over 320 million years ago, when Derbyshire lay under a warm tropical sea near the equator. Arches and caves, spires and fissures, have been carved out of the coral, creating this fascinating peak. You can see why it's sometimes known as the Dragon's Back.

There's a steep downhill section to do before the climb, then the footpath seems to take a timid line along the west side. Just as you think you've missed the summit path, the one you're on turns left and climbs for the sky. The path doesn't always keep to the crest, but avoids mild scrambles by plotting a devious course round the top rocks. Experienced walkers with a head for heights may well prefer to 'ride the dragon's back'.

From the top, Parkhouse Hill captures your attention. It's not unlike Chrome Hill, but it hasn't got a path yet. So our route descends to the little road at its foot, and takes a good look before following a pleasant farm track into Hollinsclough. On summer Sundays they serve tea and cakes in the village hall,

Left: Parkhouse Hill, Peak District National Park (Walk 31)

a nice break before heading back across Hollinsclough Rake. The path comes to this shady corner between three hills and by the confluence of two brooks. There's a fine old packhorse bridge to cross, and the cobbled Leycote track takes you uphill to the next field path. The paths round here are not well used, but they're pretty ones, through woodland and across fields of wild flowers. Farm tracks and a narrow country lane make the last bit of this journey easy.

WALK 26 DIRECTIONS

❶ From the car park cross the main road and descend the lane opposite. At the first right-hand bend turn left to take the left of two farm tracks, descending to

cross the Cistern's Clough bridge heading for Fairthorn Farm. Past the house swing left on the drive up to the road at Thirkelow Rocks.

❷ Turn right along the road for 200yds (183m), then take the farm track on the right, heading south past Thirkelow Farm. Take the right fork into he clough.

3 Where the track ends, veer slightly right to the waymarking posts highlighting a duckboard bridge and the continuing route towards Booth Farm.

4 Keep to the left of the farm and go over some steps in the wall ahead. After crossing a small field, turn left along the farm road, then fork right for Stoop Farm. Turn left along a waymarked field path, bypassing the farmhouse and climbing to a footpath intersection at the top wall. Take the path signposted Glutton Bridge via Chrome Hill.

5 Drop down to a stile and follow a wallside path that eventually climbs left to the crest before continuing over the summit, and descending to the lane beneath the conical shape of Parkhouse Hill.

6 Turn right to walk along the lane, then right again to follow a farm track. Take the left fork to reach a surfaced road, just short of Hollinsclough. Walk through the village, going right at the junction, then cross over a stile on the right. Take the higher left fork that traverses Hollinsclough Rake.

7 On reaching the green zig-zag track at Moor Side, descend right to pass a ruin and continue up a narrow valley. Cross the stream and go over the stile to reach an old packhorse bridge. Across the bridge take a stony track climbing towards the farm buildings at Leycote. On a sharp right-hand bend go left through a gate and follow a narrow path heading north-west into a wooded clough.

8 Follow the path across the simple slab bridge and climb up through the bracken towards Brand End. Go right at the fork at the top. The path becomes a more obvious track, passing Brand End Cottage and descending to the ruins of Brand End Farm.

9 Turn left up the bank by a wall here, passing to the left of another farm. Turn left along a farm track to Brand Top. Here the road leads you back to Axe Edge.

WALK 27

Through Monsal Dale, the Valley of the Gods

Following the ever-changing River Wye from Ashford-in-the-Water through lovely Monsal Dale.

DISTANCE 5.5 miles (8.8km)   **MINIMUM TIME** 3hrs 30min

ASCENT/GRADIENT 656ft (200m) ▲▲▲   **LEVEL OF DIFFICULTY** +++

PATHS Well-defined paths and tracks throughout, lots of stiles

LANDSCAPE Limestone dales and high pasture

SUGGESTED MAP OS Explorer OL24 White Peak

START / FINISH Grid reference: SK 194696

DOG FRIENDLINESS Livestock in Monsal Dale, dogs should be on lead

PARKING Ashford-in-the-Water car park

PUBLIC TOILETS At car park

The Wye is a chameleon among rivers. Rising as a peaty stream from Axe Edge, it rushes downhill, only to be confined by the concrete and tarmac of Buxton, a spa town, and the quarries to the east. Beyond Chee Dale it gets renewed vigour and cuts a deep gorge through beds of limestone, finally to calm down again among the gentle fields and hillslopes of Bakewell. The finest stretch of the river valley must be around Monsal Head, and the best approach is that from Ashford-in-the-Water, one of Derbyshire's prettiest villages found just off the busy A6.

Monsal Dale

After passing through Ashford's streets the route climbs to high pastures that give no clue as to the whereabouts of Monsal Dale. But suddenly you reach the last wall and the ground falls away into a deep wooded gorge. John Ruskin was so taken with this beauty that he likened it to the Vale of Tempe: 'you might have seen the Gods there morning and evening – Apollo and the sweet Muses of light – walking in fair procession on the lawns of it and to and fro among the pinnacles of its crags'.

The Midland Railway

It's just a short walk along the rim to reach one of Derbyshire's best-known viewpoints, where the Monsal Viaduct spans the gorge. Built in 1867 as part of the Midland Railway's line to Buxton, the five-arched, stone-built viaduct is nearly 80ft (25m) high. But the building of this railway angered Ruskin. He continued, 'you blasted its rocks away, heaped thousands of tons of shale into its lovely stream. The valley is gone and the Gods with it'.

The line closed in 1968 and the rails were ripped out, leaving only the trackbed and the bridges. Ironically, today's conservationists believe that those are worth saving and have slapped a conservation order on the viaduct. The trackbed is used as a recreational route for walkers and cyclists – the Monsal Trail. The walk continues over the viaduct, giving bird's-eye views of the river and the lawn-like surrounding pastures. It then descends to the river bank, following it westwards beneath the prominent peak of Fin Cop. The valley curves like a sickle, while the path weaves in and out of thickets, and by wetlands where tall bulrushes and irises grow. After crossing the A6 the route takes you into the mouth of Deep Dale then the shade of Great Shacklow Wood. Just past some pools filled with trout there's an entrance to the Magpie Mine Sough. The tunnel was built in 1873 to drain the Magpie Lead Mines at nearby Sheldon. Magpie was worked intermittently for over 300 years before finally closing in the 1960s. It's believed to be haunted by the ghosts of miners from the neighbouring Redsoil Mine who tragically died underground in a dispute with the Magpie men.

Looking back on the beauty of the day's walk it's hard to believe that the gods haven't returned, or at least given the place a second look.

WALK 27 DIRECTIONS

❶ From Ashford-in-the-Water car park, walk out to the road and turn right to walk along Vicarage Lane. After 100yds (91m), a footpath on the left doubles back left, then swings sharp right to continue along a ginnel behind a row of houses. Beyond a stile the path enters a field.

❷ Head for a stile in the top left corner, then veer slightly right to locate a stile allowing the route to go on to Pennyunk Lane. This walled stony track winds among high pastures. At its end go left uphill along a field edge. At the top it joins another track, heading north (right) towards the rim of Monsal Dale. The path runs along the top edge of the deep wooded dale to reach the car park at Monsal Head.

3 Take the path marked 'Viaduct and Monsal Trail' here – this way you get to walk across the viaduct. On the other side of the viaduct go through a gate on the left. Ignore the path climbing west up the hillside, but descend south-west on a grassy path raking through scrub woods down into the valley. This shouldn't be confused with the steep eroded path plummeting straight down to the foot of the viaduct.

4 Now you walk down the pleasant valley. The right of way is well away from the river at first but most walkers trace the river bank to emerge at Lees Bottom and a roadside stile.

5 Cross the A6 with great care and go through the White Lodge car park on the path the other side, where the route back to Ashford begins. Beyond the gate carry on along the path, ignoring the turning to Toddington. Go over a wall stile and then up to a rocky path, forking left for the path into Great Shacklow Wood, signposted 'Ashford'.

WHAT TO LOOK FOR

Ashford's much-photographed 17th-century Sheepwash Bridge over the River Wye was built on the original site of the ford that gave the village its name. On the far side of the bridge are the enclosures where the sheep were gathered for washing. The square-towered Norman Church of Holy Trinity has an interesting 'black marble' tympanium over the door. The marble is an impure local limestone, which becomes shiny and black when polished.

6 The path now climbs steeply through the trees and stony ground to another gate. Ignore the turning right for Sheldon and continue straight ahead, following a fine ledge path along the steep wooded slopes. Eventually the path comes down to the river, past an old mill, before joining a minor road at the bottom of Kirk Dale.

7 Turn left along the road, down to the A6 and turn right towards Ashford. Leave the road to cross Sheepwash Bridge. Turn right along Church Street, then left along Court Lane to the car park.

WHERE TO EAT AND DRINK

The Monsal Head Hotel Stables bar serves a wide variety of bar meals. So does the popular Bulls Head in Ashford, which is a Robinsons House and a traditional village pub.

WHILE YOU'RE THERE

Bakewell, next door to Ashford, is well worth a visit. The spired church of All Saints looks down on this bustling town, which is built round a fine 14th-century bridge over the River Wye. The 13th-century church was refurbished in Victorian times but has many interesting monuments, including one in the Vernon Chapel dedicated to Sir George Vernon, 'King of the Peak'. In the churchyard are two Saxon preaching crosses. The famous Bakewell Pudding Shop is also a popular venue for those who want to taste the real thing.

Chatsworth Park and Gardens

A stroll along the River Derwent past gardens and through parkland created by 18th-century landscape guru Lancelot 'Capability' Brown.

DISTANCE *7 miles (11.3km)* MINIMUM TIME *3hrs 30min*

ASCENT/GRADIENT *459ft (140m)* ▲▲▲ LEVEL OF DIFFICULTY +++

PATHS *Good paths and forest trails*

LANDSCAPE *Parkland, woodland and moorland*

SUGGESTED MAP *OS Explorer OL24 White Peak*

START / FINISH *Grid reference: SK 251699*

DOG FRIENDLINESS *Suitable for dogs, but keep on lead near livestock*

PARKING *Endensor village*

PUBLIC TOILETS *At Chatsworth*

Sitting on the banks of the River Derwent, surrounded by lush green parkland, moors and a backdrop of wooded hillsides, Chatsworth is one of the most elegant and popular of England's stately homes. First opened to the public in 1844 it continues to attract large numbers of visitors.

Bess of Hardwick

Work first started on the house in 1549 when Sir William Cavendish acquired the land and set about building a mansion. He died before it was completed and it was finished by his widow, Bess of Hardwick, who by the simple expedient of marrying four times, each time to a more powerful and richer man, succeeded in becoming the richest woman in England after the queen. She also had built the magnificent Elizabethan house of Hardwick Hall, some 15 miles (24km) to the east and now in the care of the National Trust. Bess left Chatsworth to her son Henry Cavendish, who sold it to his brother William, the 1st Earl of Devonshire. It has now been home to 14 generations of the Cavendish family and is the seat of the current Duke and Duchess of Devonshire.

Initially a three-storey Elizabethan mansion, the house has been significantly altered and added to over the centuries. The 4th Earl, who was later made 1st Duke of Devonshire for his support of William III in the 'Glorious Revolution' of 1688, practically rebuilt it. Towards the end of the 18th century the 4th Duke had the magnificent baroque stables built and engaged the services of the famous landscape gardener Lancelot 'Capability' Brown. Brown dramatically altered the 100-acre (40ha) garden that the 1st Duke had created in the 1690s and laid out the 1,000-acre (450ha) park surrounding the house. Magnificent as Chatsworth House is, it is the gardens and parkland that draw visitors back again and again. There are rare trees, sculptures, fountains and gardens, as well as a maze and adventure playground for children.

Impressive Fountain

The Emperor Fountain in the long canal pond, built in 1844 by Chatsworth's head gardener Joseph Paxton, is the highest gravity-fed fountain in the world. He designed a 9-acre (3.6ha) lake in the hills above the garden to store water

CHATSWORTH

for the fountain. On its journey down half a mile (800m) of pipe to the garden it drops 381ft (116m). Paxton also built a great conservatory at Chatsworth and went on to design the Crystal Palace for the Great Exhibition in London in 1851. Knighted by Queen Victoria, he later became a Member of Parliament and is buried in the churchyard at Edensor.

Edensor was mentioned in the Domesday Book but the 4th Duke had the original village demolished because some of the houses interfered with his view. He rebuilt it as a model village, using local stone, with each building in a different architectural style. It's still home to estate workers and pensioners.

WALK 28 DIRECTIONS

❶ From Edensor village cross the B6012 and take the footpath at the right-hand side of the large tree. Walk across the parkland to join the main drive to Chatsworth House. Just before the bridge, cross over the road and walk downhill to the river bank.

❷ Follow the River Derwent past a couple of weirs and the remains of an old mill to the next bridge

CHATSWORTH

that carries the B6012 over the river. To the left of the bridge a metal kissing gate allows access to the road. Cross the bridge.

WHILE YOU'RE THERE

Visit Edensor church, rebuilt in 1869 but containing the remnants of its 14th-century predecessor including the monuments to William and Henry Cavendish, the sons of Bess of Hardwick. Also buried within the church is Lord Frederick Cavendish who was Irish Secretary in Gladstone's government when he was hacked to death in Phoenix Park, Dublin in 1882, along with his Under-Secretary Thomas Burke, by a group of extreme Irish nationalists called the Invincibles.

3 Ignore the left turn into the drive past a gatehouse to the estate but take the next immediate left along the side of the gatehouse and continue uphill, past a house on the right and then a farm, and cross the stile on the left.

4 Cross the field, go over the next stile and then go diagonally left, uphill following the waymarkers on a well-defined path. When this meets a broad track at the top go left, cross the

WHAT TO LOOK FOR

Kathleen Kennedy, sister of American President John F Kennedy, is also buried in Edensor churchyard. She became the wife of the 10th Duke's eldest son in 1944, four months before he was killed in action in the Second World War. Had he lived he would have succeeded as the 11th Duke in 1950. Kathleen died in a plane crash in 1948. President Kennedy visited her grave in 1963, five months before he was assassinated.

WHERE TO EAT AND DRINK

Chatsworth's dining options are set out around the attractive courtyard on the east side of James Paine's 18th-century stable buildings. The Carriage House, enclosed by glass walling, offers an excellent choice of meals in a self-service, fully licensed, restaurant. Light refreshments are available in the nearby Jean Pierre's Bar.

wall into the estate by a high stile and continue to a crossroads.

5 Go straight ahead and follow the track as it passes the Swiss Lake on the right and then loops round Emperor Lake on the left. When you reach a crossroads with a tarmac lane turn left for the Hunting Tower.

6 Continue on the tarmac track as it loops left around the tower, ignoring the turn off to the right. It heads downhill, past what appears to be the remains of an old viaduct with water cascading from the end, then doubles back, still going downhill eventually reaching the car park at Chatsworth House.

7 Go past the wooden hut at the entrance to the car park and turn right on to the estate road heading north. Follow this past several wooden sculptures until you are within site of the gates at the end of the estate.

8 Near here turn left across the park to a gate that leads eventually to Baslow. Don't go through the gate but turn left on to the trail that follows the river back to Chatsworth. Turn right on to the road, cross the bridge then go immediately right on the track which leads back to the start in Edensor village.

Linacre's Peaceful Retreat from Chesterfield

Three reservoirs secreted between the Chatsworth moors and Chesterfield.

WALK 29

DISTANCE *5 miles (8km)* MINIMUM TIME *3hrs*

ASCENT/GRADIENT *820ft (250m)* ▲▲▲ LEVEL OF DIFFICULTY ✦✦✦

PATHS *Generally good paths and farm lanes, field paths can be muddy at times of high rainfall*

LANDSCAPE *Wooded valley and pastured hillsides*

SUGGESTED MAP *OS Explorer OL24 White Peak*

START / FINISH *Grid reference: SK 336727*

DOG FRIENDLINESS *Farmland, dogs should be kept under close control*

PARKING *Linacre Woods car park*

PUBLIC TOILETS *Near car park by Ranger's office*

It's easy to forget, as you look across Linacre and the valley of Holme Brook today, that Chesterfield is only a few miles away. This tranquil combe is sheltered from the west winds by the high Pennine heather moors. Three reservoirs are surrounded by attractive woodland. Linacre means arable land where flax is grown and, as early as the 13th century, linen from that flax was manufactured in the valley. But until the mid-19th century this was no more than an agricultural backwater of north-east Derbyshire.

Good Supply

It was the growth of Chesterfield and the Derbyshire coalfields, and the need for water, that brought the valley to notice. Here was a good supply, well fed by those moors to the east. The reservoirs were built one by one between 1855 and 1904 in an attempt to supply these ever-growing requirements. Until 1909, when they built the filter beds, water was pumped direct from the reservoirs to consumers' homes. According to the information sign at Linacre Reservoir the 'water supply was such that the poor used it as soup, the middle class for washing their clothes and the elite for watering their gardens'.

If you've parked on the middle car park, you're standing above the ruins of two great buildings. Not much is known about the older Linacre Hall other than its mention in old charters, but the three-storey mansion of Linacre House was once home to Dr Thomas Linacre (1460 to1524), who was president of the Royal College of Surgeons and physician to both Henry VIII and the young Mary, Queen of Scots.

Some steps take you down to the dam of the middle reservoir, and through peaceful Linacre Wood. Although many conifers have been planted for the protection of the reservoirs, about two thirds of the trees are broad-leaved, mainly sycamore, beech, oak and ash. The remaining third are larch, pine and spruce. Hidden in the woods you may discover the remains of some old Q-holes. These were crudely dug pits of about 5ft (1.5m) diameter where timber was once burnt for use in the smelting of lead ore. This was a widespread practice in the 17th century.

Beyond the reservoirs the route climbs out through a wooded clough passing the hillside hamlet of Wigley before descending into the next valley by the ancient track of Bagthorpe Lane. Frith Hall near the valley bottom has a large medieval cruck-framed barn.

The route climbs back out of the valley to Old Brampton. This straggling village is dominated by the broad-spired tower of the 14th-century parish Church of St Peter and St Paul. The oak doors came from the chapel of Derwent Hall before it was submerged beneath Ladybower Reservoir (see Walk 15). Take a look at the clock. Can you notice the mistake? It has 63 minutes painted on its face. That gives you a bit more time to stroll down a walled lane to get back to Linacre Wood.

WALK 29 DIRECTIONS

1 From the bottom of the lowest car park go down the steps into the woods. After about 100yds (91m) turn right along a waymarked bridleway heading westwards, high above the lower reservoir. Ignore the path going off to the left, which goes to the dam of the middle reservoir, but continue on the wide bridleway along the north shore of the middle reservoir.

② Take the right fork on a footpath raking up to the top end of the woods, high above the upper reservoir's dam. The path continues westwards, dipping to one of the reservoir's inlets. Cross over the lower of two bridges and then follow a well-defined concessionary footpath along the lovely shoreline.

③ On reaching the end of the reservoir ignore the left turn over the Birley Brook footbridge, but head west on the waymarked footpath. This soon leaves the woods via a ladder stile and goes straight on through scrub woodland and along the foot of an open slope.

④ Go left over a wooden footbridge and then cross a stone slab over the brook, and go straight on. A muddy path now climbs through more woods before emerging in fields north of Wigley Hall Farm. It passes to the right of the farm to a tarmac lane in the small hamlet of Wigley. Follow the lane to a crossroads.

⑤ Turn left towards Old Brampton. Just beyond the Royal Oak pub turn right down a tarmac bridleway, Bagthorpe Lane, following it past Bagthorpe Farm. The lane, now unsurfaced, descends into the valley of the

River Hipper, passing through the farmyard of Frith Hall, down to the river bridge. A winding surfaced track climbs to Westwick Lane, where you should turn left.

⑥ Just before Broomhall Farm, descend left on another track down to the river, then continue up the other side of the valley into Old Brampton.

⑦ Turn left along the lane, passing the George and Dragon pub and the church, before turning right by a telephone kiosk. The cart track descends to the top edge of Linacre Wood, then swings to the right.

⑧ At a junction of paths turn left and descend to the dam. At the far side of the dam turn left on the metalled lane, passing the public conveniences and ranger's office and climb back to the car park.

Flash Money

Rogues and vagabonds, counterfeiters and bare knuckle fighters meet the righteous in Britain's highest village.

DISTANCE 6 miles (9.7km) **MINIMUM TIME** 4hrs

ASCENT/GRADIENT 656ft (200m) ▲▲▲ **LEVEL OF DIFFICULTY** ✦✦✦

PATHS Some on road but mostly footpaths which can be boggy in wet weather

LANDSCAPE Hills, moorland and meadows

SUGGESTED MAP OS Explorer OL24 White Peak

START / FINISH Grid reference: SK 026672

DOG FRIENDLINESS Suitable for dogs, but keep on lead near livestock

PARKING On roadside near school

PUBLIC TOILETS None on route

At an altitude of 1,518ft (463m), the village of Flash proclaims itself as the 'Highest Village in Britain', and at this elevation winter comes early and lingers past the point where spring has visited its lower neighbours. Winters here can be cold. Once, during wartime, it got so cold that the vicar had icicles on his ears when he ventured from his house to the church. On another occasion a visiting minister arrived by motorcycle, much to the astonishment of the congregation. They were surprised to see him because heavy snow was imminent. They told him to watch for it falling at the window opposite his pulpit and that, should he see any, he should stop the service and depart immediately. Just after he left, it started to snow and within 20 minutes the village was cut off.

Sharp Practice

Despite being a devout community, Flash also has the dubious honour of giving its name to sharp practice. The terms 'flash money' and 'flash company' entered the English language as a consequence of events in Flash. A group of peddlers living near the village travelled the country hawking ribbons, buttons and goods made in nearby Leek. Known as 'Flash men' they initially paid for their goods with hard cash but after establishing credit, vanished with the goods and moved on to another supplier. Their name became associated with ne'er-do-wells in taverns, who helped people drink their money and were never seen again, as typified in the 18th-century English folk-song, *Flash Company*.

> *Fiddling and dancing were all my delight*
> *But keeping flash company has ruined me quite*

Beyond the Law

Flash money on the other hand referred to counterfeit bank notes, manufactured in the 18th century by a devious local gang using button presses. They were captured when a servant girl exposed them to the authorities. Some of the gang members were hanged at Chester.

FLASH

Flash was the ideal location for avoiding the law because of its proximity to the borders of three counties and police in one county could not pursue miscreants into another. At a local beauty spot called Three Shire Heads, about a mile (1.6km) north-west of the village, by a packhorse bridge, is the meeting place of Derbyshire, Cheshire and Staffordshire. Illegal bare knuckle fights were held here and when the police arrived, the participants simply crossed the bridge and continued their bout on the other side.

While all this lawlessness was going on the more peaceable inhabitants formed the Tea Pot Club. Originally a fund to help members who were sick, the Flash Loyal Union Society still has an annual Tea Pot Parade, each June from the church to Flash Bar. Tea is served in the church hall and the person pulling the most grotesque face in the gurning competition wins a teapot.

WALK 30 DIRECTIONS

❶ Walk through the village, pass the pub and an old chapel. Turn right at a footpath sign and head towards the last house. Go over a stile, turn right and follow the path over two walls. Veer left towards a gate in the corner of the field to a lane between walls. Cross another stile then turn left at a waymarker.

FLASH

2 Continue through a gate then follow the waymarker right and uphill to Wolf Edge. Pass the rocks, veer left downhill over a stile and across heather moorland. Cross a stile on the right and continue downhill to a marker post. Cross the wall, then a bridge and turn left on to the road. Go right at the junction and follow this road through Knotbury then, after the last house on the left, take the path on the left, crossing several stiles over the moorland.

3 Follow this path downhill, go left along a farm track, then resume the downward route through fields and join another track. Veer right of the road at the next waymarker, cross a stile then keep straight ahead at the next signpost. Follow this track until it crosses a bridge, then heads uphill.

WHERE TO EAT AND DRINK

The Travellers' Rest at Flash Bar is the best place in the area. Walkers can be assured a warm welcome and can relax in front of a fire with a pint of real ale, enjoying the ambience of this fine old building with it's flag floors and oak beams.

4 Opposite Spring Head turn right on to the road. At the junction, turn right then left through a gap stile. Go downhill, over a bridge, then uphill following the path, left across the field, through a gap stile and turn left on the road.

WHILE YOU'RE THERE

Visit Buxton, England's highest market town. Founded by the Romans after they discovered a hot spring in AD 79 it became a spa town in the 18th century. The elegant Crescent is modelled on Bath's Royal Crescent and the street fountain here is still fed from St Ann's Well. There are many fine buildings and not to be missed are the Pavilion Gardens with an iron and glass pavilion fronted by formal gardens.

5 Go left at the next signpost, following the waymarked path to a farm track. At some farm buildings go through a gate and then fork right. Continue to the road, cross it then continue on the path through Little Hillend. Follow this waymarked path to Adders Green Farm.

6 Turn left, through a gate and along a wall. At the end of the wall turn left, follow the wall, cross a gate and then follow the path round the foot of the hill and through a gate to Flash Bottom. Go through a small gate, turn left and up to the driveway.

7 Go through a gate opposite, follow the path over a field and up steps to the road. Turn right, then right again at the next sign. Cross several fields on a well waymarked path towards farm buildings. Cross over a stream then head uphill to the left to rejoin the road back to Flash.

WHAT TO LOOK FOR

Look for evidence of the network of packhorse trails on the moors. These routes were used from medieval times to transport goods between communities. Packhorse trains could have anything up to 50 horses and were led by a man called a 'jagger' (their ponies were Galloway cross-breeds called Jaegers). Today you will find their paved routes, descending into the valleys in distinctive 'hollow ways' or sunken lanes. Jaggers drove their beasts across the moors until the early 19th century, when canal transport finally usurped them.

Peak Practice

Ramble over hills and dales in the footsteps of one of television's favourite doctors.

DISTANCE 6 miles (9.7km)   **MINIMUM TIME** 4hrs

ASCENT/GRADIENT 459ft (140m) ▲▲▲   **LEVEL OF DIFFICULTY** ✦✦✦

PATHS Some on road otherwise good footpaths, can be muddy

LANDSCAPE Valleys, hills and meadows

SUGGESTED MAP OS Explorer OL24 White Peak

START / FINISH Grid reference: SK 089649

DOG FRIENDLINESS Suitable for dogs but keep on lead near livestock

PARKING Longnor village square

PUBLIC TOILETS Longnor village square

Longnor, a charming Peak village, situated on a high ridge between the Dove and Manifold rivers, developed as a meeting place on the ancient trade routes that once crossed these hills from Sheffield, Chesterfield, Nottingham and the Potteries. More recently it has become famous as the location of the television drama *Peak Practice*, which chronicles the everyday lives of a group of country doctors and their patients. First screened in 1993, the series put Peak District scenery on the television map and has attracted countless visitors. The earlier episodes took many different parts of the area to establish fictional Cardale — particularly Crich (see Walk 46). However, the drama has finally established a base in this little Staffordshire village to give the programmes a more permanent, community feel. Real life in Longnor, though, is somewhat quieter than the TV version, which ceased filming in 2002.

Familiar Places

There is plenty that will be familiar to viewers of *Peak Practice*. The fine brick frontage of the fictional Cardale Tearoom is actually a Georgian hotel built to serve the needs of the Crewe and Harpur Estate and still retains that name. It was used as a meeting place for the local farmers when they came to pay their annual rents at the end of March. The Horseshoe has the honour of being the TV doctors' local, the Black Swan. Dating back to 1609 it was an important staging point for the packhorse and carriage trade that crossed these hills. Ye Olde Cheshire Cheese, one of two other pubs in the village, had its origins as a cheese store in 1464. It still has a reputation for fine food but its main attraction is its resident ghost Mrs Robins, a former tenant.

The ancient pubs and cobbled market square are a reminder of Longnor's importance in days gone by as a market town. The turnpike roads with their tolls, and the lack of a railway link, prevented Longnor's development as a major trading centre, but the village retains its Victorian market hall. Now a craft centre and coffee shop, it still has the old market toll charge board, with a list of long-forgotten tariffs, above the front door. However Longnor's old world ambience and location at the heart of ancient paths ensures that it is still busy with walkers, cyclists and tourists.

LONGNOR

Local Boy

One of the highlights of a visit to Longnor is the churchyard of St Bartholomew's. Although the church is 18th century, the churchyard has some ancient graves, including that of the remarkable William Billings, who lived to the ripe old age of 112. Born in a cornfield, he was at the capture of Gibraltar in 1704, saw action at the Battle of Ramillies in 1706 and fought against the Stuarts in the Jacobite Risings of 1715 and 1745.

WALK 31 DIRECTIONS

❶ From the square take the road towards Buxton. Take the first right to turn into Church Street, and then go immediately left, up a lane and right up steps to the footpath. Follow the waymarkers, behind some houses, over a stile and along a wall. Cross another stile, go downhill and turn left on to a farm road.

2 At a fork go left then turn right on to the road. Just before the bend towards the bottom of the hill, take the farm road on the left. At the end, continue through a gate on to the footpath, through a gap stile, downhill, across a bridge and continue straight ahead. Eventually cross a stile and turn left on to the road.

3 Fork left on to a farm road, following the waymarked path. Cross a bridge by a ford and turn left to follow the river bank to the road. Turn right through Hollinsclough, following the road to the right and uphill. Turn right on to a bridleway, through a gate and downhill.

4 After 50yds (46m) fork left by two stones and continue along the flank of the hill. Cross a stile then, at a stone wall, fork left and uphill. At the top turn left at a stone gatepost, through Moorside Farm, through a kissing gate to the road. Turn right then cross a stile to a public footpath on the left.

5 Go downhill to a stream and cross a stile to the left of the ditch. Head uphill, through a stile in the wire fence, through a gap in the wall and round the field to a gap stile. Turn back towards Willshaw Farm, then left on to the well-signposted footpath towards Hill Top Farm.

6 Follow the path over stiles and past the farm to the road. Go left, then take the farm road on the right. Approaching the farm go right, steeply downhill, over a stile and follow the path along the wall. Just before the stream, cross a stile on the left and head uphill to the left of some trees.

7 Continue walking uphill, through a gate in a stone wall to some ruined buildings. Follow the track to the next farm, bear left after the barn, then go left on to a footpath uphill.

8 Go through a stile, follow the wall uphill, over two stiles to the road. Turn left then right towards Longnor. Just before the road bends left, cross a stile on the right, go downhill and over several stiles to a farm road. Turn right and follow this back to the village.

Lead Mining and the Transparent Stream

Lathkill Dale contrasts the wastes of a long-past lead-mining industry with the purity of its water.

DISTANCE *5 miles (8km)* **MINIMUM TIME** *3hrs*

ASCENT/GRADIENT *984ft (300m)* ▲▲▲ **LEVEL OF DIFFICULTY** ✦✦✦

PATHS *Generally well-defined paths. Limestone dale sides can be slippery after rain, lots of stiles*

LANDSCAPE *Partially wooded limestone dales*

SUGGESTED MAP *OS Explorer OL24 White Peak*

START / FINISH *Grid reference: SK 203657*

DOG FRIENDLINESS *Keep dogs on lead*

PARKING *Over Haddon pay car park*

PUBLIC TOILETS *At car park*

Lathkill is, by many degrees, the purest, the most transparent stream that I ever yet saw either at home or abroad...

Charles Cotton, 1676

Today, when you descend the winding lane into this beautiful limestone dale, you're confronted by ash trees growing beneath tiered limestone crags, tumbling screes, multi pastel-coloured grasslands swaying in the breeze and that same crystal clear stream, still full of darting trout.

Invasion of the Lead Miners

Yet it was not always so. In the 18th and 19th centuries lead miners came here and stripped the valley of its trees. They drilled shafts and adits into the white rock, built pump houses, elaborate aqueducts, waterwheels and tramways; and when the old schemes failed to realise profits they came up with new, even bigger ones. Inevitably nobody made any real money, and by 1870 the price of lead had slumped from overseas competition and the pistons stopped.

On this walk you will see the fading remnants of this past, juxtaposed with the natural world that is gradually reclaiming the land. In reality it's Natural England, who are managing the grasslands and woods as part of the Derbyshire Dales National Nature Reserve. Your route starts on a narrow winding lane from Over Haddon to a clapper bridge by Lathkill Lodge. A lush tangle of semi-aquatic plants surround the river and the valley sides are thick with ash and sycamore. In spring you're likely to see nesting moorhens and mallards. In the midst of the trees are some mossy pillars, the remains of an aqueduct built to supply a head of water for the nearby Mandale Mine. The path leaves the woods and the character of the dale changes again. Here sparse ash trees grow out of the limestone screes, where herb Robert adds splashes of pink.

Disappearing River

In the dry periods of summer the river may have disappeared completely beneath its permeable bed of limestone. The sun-dried soils on the southern slopes are too thin to support the humus-loving plants of the valley bottom. Instead, here you'll see the pretty early purple orchid, cowslips with their yellowy primrose-like flowers and clumps of the yellow-flowered rock rose.

After climbing out of Cales Dale the walk traverses the high fields of the White Peak plateau. If you haven't already seen them, look out for Jacob's ladder, a 3ft (1m) tall, increasingly rare plant with clusters of bell-like purple-blue flowers.

By the time you have crossed the little clapper bridge by Lathkill Lodge and climbed back up that winding lane to the car park, you'll have experienced one of Derbyshire's finest dales.

WALK 32 DIRECTIONS

① Turn right out of the car park, and descend the narrow tarmac lane, which winds down into Lathkill Dale.

② Just before reaching Lathkill Lodge and the river, turn right along a concessionary track that runs parallel to the north bank. The path passes several caves and a mineshaft as it weaves its way through woodland and thick vegetation. South of Haddon Grove the trees thin out to reveal the fine limestone crags and screes of the upper dale. The path now becomes rougher as it traverses an area of screes.

③ At a junction of routes go over the footbridge and follow a little path sneaking into Cales Dale. Take the left fork down to a stile at the valley bottom. You now join the Limestone Way long distance route on a very steep stepped path climbing eastwards out of the dale and on to the high pastures of Calling Low.

④ The path heads east of south-east across the fields then, just before Calling Low farm, diverts left (waymarked) through several small wooded enclosures. The path swings right beyond the farm,

then half left across a cow-pocked field to its top left-hand corner and some woods.

⑤ Over steps in the wall the path cuts a corner through the woods before continuing through more fields to reach a tarmac lane, where you turn left.

⑥ After about 500yds (457m), follow a signposted footpath that begins at a stile in a dry-stone wall on the left. This heads north-east across fields to a huge farming complex, Meadow Place Grange. Waymarks show the way across the cobbled courtyard, where the path continues between two stable blocks into another field.

⑦ After heading north across the field to the brow of Lathkill Dale, turn right through a gate on to a zig-zag track descending to the river. Cross the old clapper bridge to Lathkill Lodge and follow the outward route, a tarmac lane, back to the car park.

EXTENDING THE WALK
You can see the lower part of Lathkill Dale by leaving the main route at Point **Ⓐ** and descending through Youlgreave village to Alport, from where a riverside path takes you all the way back to the start, at the bottom of the hill near Over Haddon.

WALK

33

Ancient Circles, Barrows and Stones

A walk around Arbor Low, the 'Stonehenge of the North'.

DISTANCE *6 miles (9.7km)*   MINIMUM TIME *4hrs*

ASCENT/GRADIENT *492ft (150m)* ▲▲▲   LEVEL OF DIFFICULTY +++

PATHS *Mostly well-defined paths, some road walking; limestone steps in Cales Dales can be very slippery when wet; several stiles*

LANDSCAPE *Limestone dales and woodland*

SUGGESTED MAP *OS Explorer OL24 White Peak*

START / FINISH *Grid reference: SK 194645*

DOG FRIENDLINESS *Keep on lead near livestock*

PARKING *Moor Lane pay car park*

PUBLIC TOILETS *Nearest at Youlgreave*

Known as the 'Stonehenge of the North', Arbor Low is probably one of the most important prehistoric monuments in Britain. Like other mysterious stone circles no one really knows why it was built or what function it served. Various theories suggest that it may have been a giant astronomical calculator, a religious centre, a meeting place or perhaps the earliest known supermarket.

Trading Centre

Research has shown that by the late neolithic period, around about 2500 BC, complex trading networks had built up throughout Britain. Evolving from simple methods of exchange, their development mirrors the building of the henges. Throughout the Peak District axes have been discovered. These highly polished weapons were made from hard stone and originated from places as far away as North Wales, the Lake District and Northern Ireland. Arbor Low, built near well-established trading routes, might have been the trading centre for the distribution of goods like these.

The name, a corruption of the Anglo Saxon, Eorthburg Hlaw, means simply earthwork mound. It consists of a circular earthwork bank with two entrances, an internal ditch and a raised inner platform with a circle of limestone blocks. The stones may have stood upright when Arbor Low was built but nowadays they lie flat. The passage of time may have caused them to fall over or, as has been speculated, they were deliberately knocked over by people who knew their true purpose and significance and were afraid of them.

Ceremonial Site

At the centre of the circle are the fallen stones of what is known as the cove. This, the most sacred part of the site, was made up of seven stone slabs and may have been rectangular when they were erect. No one knows what rites and ceremonies were conducted here. Only initiates would have been allowed to enter, their actions concealed from everyone else by the strategic placing of two of the larger stone slabs. Perhaps human sacrifice took place on this spot.

During excavations the skeleton of a man was discovered in the cove, lying on its back and surrounded by blocks of stone when the usual form of burial from that period had the knees drawn up.

Gib Hill

Across the field from Arbor Low lies a long barrow with a round one built on top of it. The name Gib Hill suggests that it was once used for a gibbet, probably in the Middle Ages. Recent research indicates that it may have been a site of execution further back in time. In the Dark Ages people feared places like Arbor Low. New, emerging rulers, anxious to establish their power found that one way to do it was to organise executions in such places of local superstition.

WALK 33

WALK 33 DIRECTIONS

1 Exit the car park on Moor Lane, turn left and then follow the road to the Y-junction. Cross the road, go through the gap in the wall, through a kissing gate and follow the well-defined path across the field.

2 Go over two wall stiles and continue following the path. Cross a fence by another stile and continue to the wall at the edge of the wood. Go through a kissing gate into Low Moor Wood.

WHILE YOU'RE THERE

Visit Bakewell, one of the most charming towns in Derbyshire. There's a fascinating 8th-century Saxon cross in the churchyard with carvings illustrating the Crucifixion and Annunciation. There are also several late Saxon and Norman stones that are worth a look. They are probably from a much earlier church and were brought to Bakewell by medieval masons.

3 Follow the path through the wood, go through a gate and follow the well-defined path across another field. Take the diverted path round Calling Low Farm via two kissing gates, go through a wood and three more kissing gates to get back on to open meadow.

WHAT TO LOOK FOR

Look for a low bank and ditch which stretches away from the larger of the two entrances on Arbor Low and curves towards, then behind Gib Hill. Known as The Avenue, it may have been a ceremonial link between the two sites, but more likely it is a boundary, perhaps from the Roman period.

4 Follow this path diagonally downhill and then go through further kissing gates. Continue on the path still downhill, through another gate into Lathkill Dale National Nature Reserve. Head downhill on a limestone path and steps. Cross a stile at the bottom and then head uphill on the path to your left.

WHERE TO EAT AND DRINK

The Original Bakewell Pudding Shop is situated in the square of the market town of Bakewell. This is where the famous pudding was first made and although the shop has changed hands several times since then it still produces puddings to the same secret recipe. The restaurant also serves some of the best food available in the Peak District.

5 Look out for the cave that is in the rocks on the left as you reach the top. Continue uphill, through a gate and on to the farm. Enter the farm steading via some stone steps and continue on the road, uphill between buildings until you see a signpost for Cales Farm pointing left.

6 Turn on to this farm road and follow it until it joins the main road. Turn right and then continue for 0.5 mile (800m) then turn left on to the drive for Upper Oldhams Farm, following the signs for the henge.

7 Go through the farm yard following the signs, go through a gate, turn left along a path then cross another stile to reach the henge. Retrace your steps to the main road, turn right and walk about 2.5 miles (4km) back to the car park.

Birds, Beasts and Butterflies at Tittesworth

Reservoir biodiversity provides drinking water for the Potteries and a valuable habitat for wildlife.

DISTANCE *4.5 miles (7.2km)* MINIMUM TIME *3hrs*

ASCENT/GRADIENT *131ft (40m)* ▲▲▲ LEVEL OF DIFFICULTY +++

PATHS *Good well-made footpaths, forest tracks and roads*

LANDSCAPE *Reservoir and woodland*

SUGGESTED MAP *OS Explorer OL24 White Peak*

START / FINISH *Grid reference: SK 994602*

DOG FRIENDLINESS *Suitable for dogs*

PARKING *Reservoir visitor centre (pay car park)*

PUBLIC TOILETS *At reservoir visitor centre*

Tittesworth Reservoir and dam were built in 1858 to collect water from the River Churnet and provide a reliable water supply to Leek's thriving textile and cloth-dying industry. By 1963 work to increase its size had been completed and local farmland was flooded to create a reservoir capable of supplying drinking water to Stoke-on-Trent and surrounding areas. With a capacity of 6.5 billion gallons (29.5 billion litres), when full it can supply 10 million gallons (45 million litres) of water every day.

Habitat for Wildlife

The land around the reservoir provides a habitat for a wide variety of wildlife and many creatures can be seen in the course of this walk. Look out for brown hares in the fields near the car park. You can tell them from rabbits by their very long legs, black-tipped ears and a triangular black and light brown tail. Otters were once hunted almost to extinction by dogs and although the sport is now illegal their numbers remain low. They are nocturnal creatures and not often seen, but look out for their droppings by the water's edge and the tell-tale prints of their webbed feet and wavy line tail prints in the sand and soft mud. Look also for holes in the banks along the River Churnet, where it enters the reservoir. Although he's a difficult little creature to spot, a hole may just be the entrance to a vole burrow and home to a water vole like Ratty from *The Wind in the Willows*.

Bats and Birds

Europe's smallest bat, the pipistrelle suffered a severe decline in numbers in the last decades of the 20th century due to loss of hunting habitats like hedges, ponds and grassland. Pond restoration near Churnet Bay is encouraging their return and they can best be seen here near dusk, flying at an incredible speed, twisting and turning as they dive to gobble caddisflies, moths and gnats.

Bird life around the reservoir is also abundant and there are two bird hides from which visitors can observe in comfort. Look out particularly for skylarks, small birds with a high-pitched continuous warble, that nest in the meadows around Tittesworth. The song thrush, another bird that has been in decline, also finds a home here, as does the linnet. Look especially for the male of the species in spring and summer when it has a bright blood-red breast and forehead. You'll find them in the trees and bushes near the visitor centre and at the hide near the conservation pool.

At various times of the year you might spot barnacle geese, great crested grebe, pied flycatchers, spectacular kingfishers, cormorants and even a rare osprey that has visited here several times in recent years.

WALK 34 DIRECTIONS

❶ Facing the entrance to the visitor centre turn left, cross the car park and follow the path signed 'Waymarked Walks and Play Area'. Beyond the Nature Trails

sign, continue along the concrete path around the edge of the reservoir. Cross two bridges and follow the Long Trail/Short Trail signs along a well-surfaced path. At a junction by a picnic table turn left on to a forest trail.

TITTESWORTH RESERVOIR

2 Follow the waymarked Long Trail through the wood, crossing a bridge and some duckboarding, then turn left at a T-junction again following the Long Trail (follow footprint waymarks). As the path leaves the wood fork right on to a grassy track.

3 Continue along the bank of the reservoir then re-enter woodland, cross some duckboards and rejoin the broad, hard-surface track. Cross a bridge by a picnic table, ascend some steps and continue along duckboards. Skirt the edge of a wood, keeping the fence on your left, then go downhill through a wood and along the reservoir bank.

4 Go through some more woodland, cross a bridge, walk up some steps then leave the wood and continue on a gravel path. Follow the path downhill towards the dam. Go through a gate and cross the dam head. At the far end, go uphill on a series of steps and turn right on to a footpath.

5 Go through a gate, turn right at a T-junction on to a metalled lane. Continue on this through a farm, following the signs for Meerbrook, straight ahead. At the road junction turn right at the Long Trail and Visitor Centre sign. Turn right again following the pedestrian-only road to Tittesworth Reservoir. When this turns to the right, bear left on a footpath beside the reservoir.

6 Go through a gate on to the road then turn right into the public entrance to the reservoir to return to the visitor centre.

Overleaf: The Roaches Hill with Hen Cloud behind, Staffordshire (Walk 35)

Lud's Church and the Roaches

Follow Sir Gawain and find the chapel of the Green Knight.

WALK 35

DISTANCE 6.75 miles (10.9km) **MINIMUM TIME** 4hrs

ASCENT/GRADIENT 1,020ft (311m) ▲▲▲ **LEVEL OF DIFFICULTY** ✦✦✦

PATHS Rocky moorland paths, forest tracks and road

LANDSCAPE Moor and woodland

SUGGESTED MAP OS Explorer OL24 White Peak

START / FINISH Grid reference: SK 005621

DOG FRIENDLINESS Keep on lead near livestock

PARKING In lay-by on lane near Windygates Farm

PUBLIC TOILETS None on route

The jagged ridge of the Roaches is one of the most popular outdoor locations in the Peak District National Park. The name is a corruption of the French for rocks – roches. It was here on the gritstone crags that the 'working class revolution' in climbing took place in the 1950s. Manchester lads, Joe Brown, a builder, and Don Whillans, a plumber, went on to become legends within the climbing fraternity by developing new rock climbing techniques wearing gym shoes and using Joe's mother's discarded clothes line as a rope. Other, less tangible legends, surround this long outcrop, several of them attached to Doxey Pool. Locals speak in hushed voices of a young mermaid, who lived in the pool but was captured by a group of men. If the stories are to be believed her ghost can still be heard singing through the mist. Lurking in the darkest depths of the pool is Jenny Greenteeth, a hideous monster with green skin, long hair and sharp teeth, who grabs the ankles of anyone unfortunate enough to get too close, dragging them to a watery grave.

Sir Gawain and the Green Knight

But the greatest legend associated with the Roaches is the Arthurian tale of *Sir Gawain and the Green Knight*. According to the 14th-century poem a knight on horseback, cloaked entirely in green, gatecrashed a feast at Camelot and challenged the Knights of the Round Table. Sir Gawain rose to the challenge and beheaded the Green Knight but the latter retrieved his head and laughingly challenged Sir Gawain to meet with him again, in a year's time, at the Green Chapel. This has been identified as Lud's Church, near the Roaches. In the 1950s Professor Ralph Elliot, now of the University of Adelaide in Australia, identified the Roaches as the general location of the chapel from the text.

> Great crooked crags, cruelly jagged, the bristling barbs of rock
> seemed to brush the sky

Professor Elliot's theory was supported by a group of linguists, working on the poem at the same time, who placed the work in the same 15-mile (25km) radius. The professor and a group of students from Keele University, where he

THE ROACHES

was then based, tramped all over the countryside looking for a suitable cave to match the poetic description.

> *A hole in each end and on either side,*
> *And overgrown with grass and great patches*
> *All hollow it was within, only an old cavern*
> *Or the crevice of an ancient crag*

Lud's Church fitted the bill. This rocky cleft was created by a mass of sandstone slipping away from the slope of the hill. It was here that Sir Gawain kept his rendezvous with the Green Knight resulting in that ghostly gentleman losing his head for a second time.

WALK 35 DIRECTIONS

❶ From the lane go through the main gate by the interpretation panel and follow the path half right to the end of the rocks. At a gate in the wall on your right, turn left and straight uphill on a rocky track. Go left through a pair of stone gateposts and continue right on a well-defined track.

❷ The path is flanked by rocks on the right and woodland to the left and below. Follow it to the right and uphill through a gap in the rocks. Turn left and then continue uphill. Continue following this ridge path. Pass to the left of Doxey Pool and on towards the trig point.

❸ From here descend on a paved path, past the Bearstone Rock to join the road at Roach End. Go

through a gap in the wall, over a stile and follow the path uphill keeping the wall on the left. At the signpost fork right on to the concessionary path to Danebridge.

❹ Follow this path keeping straight ahead at a crossroads, go through a wall gate and up towards an outcrop. Carry on along the ridge then head down to a signpost by a gate. Turn right and follow the bridleway signed 'Gradbach'. At the next signpost fork right towards Lud's Church.

❺ After exploring Lud's Church continue along the path, through woodland, following the signs for Roach End, eventually taking a paved path uphill. Keep the wall on your left-hand side and at the top, cross a stile on to the gated road and follow this back to the lay-by near Windygates Farm.

Pilsbury Castle and the Upper Dove Valley

The upper valley of the Dove has quiet villages and historic remains.

DISTANCE *7.5 miles (12.1km)* **MINIMUM TIME** *4hrs*

ASCENT/GRADIENT *804ft (245m)* ▲▲▲ **LEVEL OF DIFFICULTY** ✦✦✦

PATHS *Field paths and lanes, some steep climbs, lots of stiles*

LANDSCAPE *Pastures, limestone valley*

SUGGESTED MAP *OS Explorer OL24 White Peak*

START / FINISH *Grid reference: SK 127603*

DOG FRIENDLINESS *Keep dogs on lead*

PARKING *Parson's Field, Hartington, pay car park*

PUBLIC TOILETS *Near car park*

Hartington, lying in the mid regions of the Dove Valley, is a prosperous village with 18th-century houses and hotels built in local limestone and lined around spacious greens. Its history can be traced back to the Normans, when it was recorded as Hartedun, the centre for the De Ferrier's estate. Hartington Hall, now the youth hostel, was first built in 1350 but was substantially rebuilt in 1611. Bonnie Prince Charlie is reputed to have stopped here in 1745 on his march into Derby, where 5,000 Highland troops were amassing to fight for the Jacobite cause. He didn't know that the Duke of Devonshire had amassed 30,000 loyalists. The Prince would retreat to Scotland, where he would be cruelly dealt with at Culloden.

As you leave the village the lane climbs past the Church of St Giles, which has a battlemented Perpendicular tower. It continues up the high valley sides of the Dove, then on through emerald high fields and valley.

Pilsbury Castle

Pilsbury Castle hides from the viewer until the very last moment, but then a grassy ramp swoops down to it from the hillsides. Only the earthworks are now visible, but you can imagine its supreme impregnable position on the limestone knoll that juts out into the valley. You can see the motte, a man-made mound built to accommodate the wooden keep, and the bailey, a raised embankment that would have had a wooden stockade round it.

The castle's exact history is disputed. It was probably built around 1100 by the Normans, on the site of an Iron Age fort. It may have been a stronghold used earlier by William I to suppress a local rebellion in his 'Wasting of the North' campaign. Being in the middle of the De Ferrier estate it was probably their administrative centre. In the 1200s this function would have been moved to Hartington.

Views up-valley are fascinating, with the conical limestone peaks of Parkhouse and Chrome Hills in the distance. Now the route descends into Dovedale for the first time, crossing the river into Staffordshire. The lane climbs to a high lane running the length of the dale's east rim. Note the change in the rock – it's now the darker gritstone. The crags of Sheen Hill have been blocking the view east, but once past them you can see for miles, across the Manifold Valley to the Roaches and Hen Cloud. A field path takes the route on its finale, descending along a line of crags with lofty views.

WALK 36 DIRECTIONS

❶ Turn left out of the car park and follow the road through the centre of the village. Turn left, uphill by the church on Hyde Lane

and then take the third path on the left. This descends northwards across fields. Just below a farmhouse, the path swings left to follow a dry-stone wall on the left.

2 The path cuts across the stony drive coming up the hill from Bank Top Farm. Waymarking posts highlight the continuing route along the high valleysides.

3 West of Carder Low (grid ref 126627) the path goes through a gateway by an intersection of walls and becomes indistinct. Here, climb half right to another gateway, then head for a group of trees. Beyond these another footpath signpost shows the way uphill to a step stile in a ridge wall, where you look down into a small valley.

4 Descend into the valley and turn left to reach a high lane by a stone barn. A stile across the road allows you on to the continuing path, rounding the high slopes above Pilsbury. The footpath rakes left down the hillslopes to a farm track and wall alongside the ancient earthworks of Pilsbury Castle. A gate in the stone wall allows further inspection.

5 Turn right and continue down a grassy track, which eventually degenerates into a field path heading up the valley towards Crowdecote.

6 Just past Bridge End Farm turn left to cross the Dove by a little footbridge. Follow the path directly uphill across a field.

7 Beyond the wall stile the path veers right, through scrub, to reach the Longnore road near Edgetop. Turn left along the high lane to Harris Close Farm.

8 A stile on the nearside of an outbuilding at Harris Close starts the path back to Hartington. In all but one field there's a wall on the right for guidance. After going through a wood, the path descends through scrub into the valley. It joins a farm track southwards towards Bridge-end farm.

9 At the signpost 'Hartington' turn left through a gate and across a field. A footbridge, hidden by trees, allows the crossing of the Dove. The intermittent path gradually swings right (south-east) across fields. The path aims for the woods to the left of the dairy and enters them via a gate. At the other side go through a field beside a dairy and turn left along the lane to return to Hartington.

Along the Manifold Way

Follow the former Manifold Valley, route of one of England's most picturesque small railways.

DISTANCE 5.5 miles (8.8km)	**MINIMUM TIME** 3hrs 30min

ASCENT/GRADIENT 518ft (158m) ▲▲▲   **LEVEL OF DIFFICULTY** +++

PATHS Hard surface on Manifold Way, other footpaths can be muddy in wet weather

LANDSCAPE Woodland, meadows and valleys

SUGGESTED MAP OS Explorer OL24 White Peak

START / FINISH Grid reference: SK 095561

DOG FRIENDLINESS Keep on lead near livestock

PARKING On Manifold Way near Wetton Mill

PUBLIC TOILETS Next to Wetton Mill Tea Room

Described by one local as 'A line starting nowhere and ending up at the same place', the, narrow gauge Leek and Manifold Valley Light Railway was one of England's most picturesque white elephants. Though it survived a mere 30 years from its first run in June 1904, its legacy is still enjoyed today. It ran for 8 miles (12.9km) from Hulme End to Waterhouses where passengers and freight had to transfer to the standard gauge Leek branch of the North Staffordshire Railway.

The Leek and Manifold Valley Light Railway

The narrow gauge railway owed its existence to Leek businessmen who feared that their town would lose out because of the newly opened Buxton-to-Ashbourne line. Their solution was to provide a local rail link to the south-east of the county. For the entire period of its existence the railway was a financial disaster and should probably never have been built. It was only made possible because the Light Railways Act of 1896 provided grants for small projects like this and reduced bureaucracy.

A Little Bit of India in the Peaks

Engineer Everard Calthorp, who built the Barsi Railway near Bombay, used the same techniques and design of locomotive for the Leek and Manifold Valley Light Railway in the Peak District as he used in India, and as a result it looked more like a miniature Indian railway than a classic English line. The engines were painted chocolate and black and pulled carriages of primrose yellow.

Milk Train

The success of the line was, however, based on the supposition that the Ecton Copper Mines would re-open and that an extension to Buxton would tap into a lucrative tourist market. But the mines didn't re-open and the extension was never built. To survive, the small railway made a daily collection of milk from farms along the line and hauled produce from the creamery at Ecton for onward transportation to London. Passenger traffic was light, probably due to the long

MANIFOLD VALLEY

distance and steep uphill climb from the valley bottom to the villages on the top. Tourists did flock to the area on summer weekends and bank holidays, often causing severe overloading of the carriages as they headed for scenic areas like Thor's Cave and Beeston Tor. Even with this seasonal upturn the line never made a profit and when the creamery shut in 1933 it was the end of the road for the miniature trains. The last one ran on 10 March 1934.

The track was lifted and the bed presented by the railway company to Staffordshire County Council. They had the remarkable foresight and imagination to be one of the first local authorities to take a disused railway line and convert it to a pedestrian path. Today, as the Manifold Way, it is a favourite of walkers and cyclists.

WALK 37 DIRECTIONS

❶ At the road junction near the car park, take the lane signposted 'Butterton' opposite the bridge.

Just after the road bends sharply right near the ford, go through a gate on the left and walk along a valley-bottom track, with the brook on your left.

2 Beyond the new footbridge turn right at the signpost 'Fp (footpath) to Butterton' and follow this along the course of a stream to reach the village. In the final field go left, uphill, to reach the road.

3 Turn right on to the road, cross the ford and then head uphill, forking right to go past the church and the Black Lion Inn. Turn right at a T-junction, go left at a public footpath sign, cross two stiles then head along a spur, through some trees and down a steep hill to cross the stream by a wooden bridge.

4 Head uphill keeping the hedge on your left, cross two stiles and turn right on to the road. Turn left towards Eckstone then right across a stile on to the footpath.

Cross two stiles, turn right behind a small derelict building and follow the line of the wall. Cross a stile, then a stream and head uphill keeping the fence on your left.

5 At the junction where the fence meets with a stone wall, turn right, cross the field and nip over a stile by a large tree. Follow this path across a field through a gateway and ahead across marshy ground to a junction of paths in the corner of the field where the wall meets the hedge.

6 Go over a stile and keep ahead through the next field to emerge on the road by Shorecroft Barn. Turn right, then at the end, opposite the church, go left. When you reach the T-junction, turn right on to Leek Road.

7 Turn right again at the next junction, cross over the road and then walk down School Lane. Turn left through a gap stile on to a public footpath. Clamber through three more gap stiles, following the course of a stream. Enter a wooded area, go downhill, cross over a stile and then turn right to join the Manifold Way. Follow this easy, well-defined trail through an old railway tunnel, back to the car park.

In the Lair of the White Worm

Follow a fascinating limestone trail to visit the film location of Bram Stoker's last nightmare.

DISTANCE *5 miles (8km)*   MINIMUM TIME *3hrs 30min*

ASCENT/GRADIENT *423ft (129m)* ▲▲▲   LEVEL OF DIFFICULTY +++

PATHS *Forest tracks, grass and mud, hard footpath*

LANDSCAPE *Hillside, valley, meadows and woodland*

SUGGESTED MAP *OS Explorer OL24 White Peak*

START / FINISH *Grid reference: SK 085545*

DOG FRIENDLINESS *Keep on lead near livestock*

PARKING *At Grindon church*

PUBLIC TOILETS *None on route*

Anyone who has seen Ken Russell's film, *The Lair of the White Worm* (1988), will recognise at once the entrance to Thor's Cave and may, as a result, feel slightly apprehensive when climbing the path up the hillside. The opening shot in the film features the famous landmark and, as the blood red titles roll, the camera slowly zooms in towards the mouth of the cave.

Scene of a Horror Film

Based loosely on Bram Stoker's last novel, *The Lair of the White Worm* stars Amanda Donahoe, Hugh Grant, Catherine Oxenburg, Peter Capaldi and Sammi Davis. Stoker's original story was based in the Peak District in the 19th century and tells of odd disappearances, legends of a fearsome giant serpent and of the strange and sinister Lady Arabella. Film maker Russell has moved the whole story in time to the 20th century and altered the plot considerably.

A young Scottish archaeology student, Angus Flint (played by Peter Capaldi) finds a mysterious, reptilian skull at an excavation he's working on near his lodgings. Later he takes the two sisters who run the guest house to the home of Lord James D'Ampton (Hugh Grant) for the annual celebrations to commemorate the slaying of the D'Ampton Worm by his ancestor. Angus leaves early to escort one of the sisters (Mary played by Sammi Davis) home.

Passing through woods near where her parents mysteriously disappeared they encounter the sensuous and snakelike Lady Sylvia (irresistibly portrayed by Amanda Donahoe). In the dark cellars of her Gothic mansion, Temple Hall, she has been worshipping an evil and ancient snake god. It has an insatiable appetite for virgin flesh and Mary's sister Eve (Catherine Oxenburg) is on the menu. D'Ampton connects the disappearance of Eve with Lady Sylvia and, taking on his ancestor's role, heads for Thor's Cave to search for a tunnel connecting to Temple Hall. The nonsense ends in predictable fashion, with Angus emerging as the reluctant hero (wearing a kilt and playing the bagpipes), snatching Eve from the monster's jaws and slaying it with a hand grenade.

GRINDON

Thor's Cave may be the most famous cave in the Peak District but there are several others, including Ossom's Cave and Elderbush. Both have been explored and produced bones and flints from the Stone and Bronze Ages. So, Thor's Cave may have been home to one or two prehistoric beasties but in reality none of them were big white snakes. Formed over thousands of years from the combined effects of wind and rain on the soft limestone, it probably sheltered animals like giant red deer, bears or even early humans. Excavations have revealed it to be the site of a Bronze Age burial, although much of the evidence was lost by over-zealous 19th-century excavators.

WALK 38 DIRECTIONS

1 From the car park turn left, then right at the Old Rectory and head downhill. After 100 yds (91m) go left on to a public footpath, go through a gap stile, cross a field and head downhill on the right of two diverging paths. Cross a bridge, go through a gate then a gap stile and go downhill, keeping the stream and the wood on your right.

GRINDON

② When the wall heads left go through a gap stile on your right continuing downhill into National Trust land at Ladyside. Cross over a stile, go through a wood and then leave it via another stile. Turn right, still continuing downhill to reach a stile leading on to the Manifold Way.

③ Cross the Manifold Way, then a bridge and take the path uphill following the signs for Thor's Cave. At the mouth of the cave turn left, continue on a track uphill, curve right before a stile and follow the path to the summit for superb views along the Manifold Valley.

WHILE YOU'RE THERE

Well worth a visit is All Saints Church near the car park at Grindon. Known as 'the Cathedral of the Moorlands' it contains the remains of an earlier Saxon church, an ancient font and stone coffins. There's also a memorial to the airmen and journalists who died in a plane crash on Grindon Moor during the terrible winter of 1947 when attempting to bring relief supplies to the village.

④ Retrace your steps to the Manifold Way and turn left. Continue past a car park at the caravan park and bear right on the Manifold Way and then cross two bridges. At the beginning of the third bridge cross a stile on the right and follow the path back, parallel to the road and then curving left and uphill.

⑤ Go through a gate by a dried-up pond and follow the path uphill with the wall on your right. Keep straight on, through successive fields, with the church spire at Grindon ahead.

WHAT TO LOOK OUT FOR

Near the church gates is an old stone known as the Rindle Stone. It contains the inscription 'The lord of the manor of Grindon established his right to this Rindle at Staffordshire Assizes on March 17th 1862'. A Rindle is a brook that only flows in wet weather. Why anyone would want to establish legal right to such a thing is not explained on the stone.

⑥ Maintain your direction across fields, keeping to the left of the farm. Finally join a farm road, continue along a walled path, then turn right on to the road opposite Chestnut Cottage. Take the first left and follow this road back to the car park.

WHERE TO EAT AND DRINK

From the summit slope of Thor's Cave, a footpath runs eastwards across the fields for just under a mile (1.6km) to Wetton. Ye Olde Royal Oak is located in the centre of the village and has long been a popular destination for walkers. The 400-year-old pub offers a choice of decent real ales, as well as hot and cold food served daily. If the weather is fine, you can sit outside in the beer garden and relax.

Wolfscote Dale and a Railway Trail

Wolfscote Dale and Biggin Dale wind through the heart of the upland limestone country.

DISTANCE 7.5 miles (12.1km)	**MINIMUM TIME** 4hrs 30min

ASCENT/GRADIENT 557ft (170m) ▲▲▲ **LEVEL OF DIFFICULTY** ✚✚✚

PATHS Path below Blue John Mines can be tricky in wintry conditions, generally well-defined paths, limestone dale sides can be slippery after rain, quite a few stiles

LANDSCAPE Partially wooded limestone dales and high pasture

SUGGESTED MAP OS Explorer OL24 White Peak

START / FINISH Grid reference: SK 156549

DOG FRIENDLINESS Can run free on much of walk

PARKING Tissington Trail pay car park (at former Alsop Station)

PUBLIC TOILETS None on route

From its source, on Axe Edge, to Hartington the River Dove is little more than a stream, flowing almost apologetically past the Dragon's Back at Chrome Hill (see Walk 26), and in an attractive but shallow valley south of Crowdecote. But once through the pretty woodlands of Beresford Dale it gets more confident and cuts a deep limestone canyon with cliffs and tors almost equal to those of the more celebrated Dovedale. This canyon is Wolfscote Dale, and it's wilder and more unspoiled than Dovedale, with narrower, less populated paths, and less woodland to hide the crags. Weirs have been constructed along the river to create calm pools that attract trout and grayling to linger.

Compleat Angler

The river here was a joy to Charles Cotton, a 17th-century poet born in nearby Beresford Hall. Cotton, an enthusiastic young angler, introduced his great friend, Izaak Walton, to the area and taught him the art of fly-fishing (see Walk 41). Together they built a fishing temple in the nearby woods of Beresford Dale (in private grounds). They wrote *The Compleat Angler*, a collection of fishing stories published in 1651. Unfortunately Cotton's precarious financial position forced him to sell the hall in 1681, and it now lies in a ruinous state.

The path up Wolfscote Dale begins at Lode Mill, which still has its waterwheel intact. The river, verged by lush vegetation, has cut a deep and twisting valley through the limestone. The slopes are thickly wooded with ash, sycamore and alder. Further north this woodland thins out to reveal more of the crags, and a ravine opens out to the right of Coldeaton Bridge. The dale, like so many in Derbyshire, is rich in wildlife. Dippers, pied wagtails and grey wagtails often forage along the limestone banks, and if you're quick enough you may see the blue flash of a kingfisher diving for a fish. The dale divides again beneath the magnificent Peaseland Rocks. It's a shame to leave the Dove but Biggin Dale is a pleasing contrast. For most of the year it's a dry valley, but in winter the rocky path may be jostling for room with a newly surfaced stream. It's a narrow dale with limestone screes and scrub gorse. What looks like a natural cave on the right is in fact the entrance to an old lead mine. Through a gate you enter a National Nature Reserve, known for its many species of limestone-loving plants and its butterflies. At the top of the dale you come to Biggin, a straggling village, from where the return route is an easy-paced one, using the Tissington Trail, which ambles over the high plains of Alsop Moor.

WALK 39

WALK 39 DIRECTIONS

1 From the car park, cross the busy A515 road and follow Milldale Road immediately opposite. After a junction you are offered a parallel footpath on the left, keeping you away and safe from the traffic.

2 On reaching the bottom of the dale by Lode Mill, turn right along the footpath, tracing the river's east bank through a winding, partially wooded valley.

3 Ignore the footpath on the right at Coldeaton Bridge, but instead stay with Wolfscote Dale beneath thickly wooded slopes on the right. Beyond a stile the woods cease and the dale becomes bare and rock-fringed, with a cave on the right and the bold pinnacles of Peaseland Rocks ahead. Here the valley sides open out into the dry valley of Biggin Dale, where this route goes next.

4 The signposted path into Biggin Dale begins beyond a stile in a cross-wall and climbs by that wall. It continues through scrub woodland and beneath limestone screes. Beyond a gate you enter a nature reserve.

5 There's another gate at the far end of the nature reserve. Beyond it the dale curves left and then right, before dividing again beneath the hill pastures of Biggin

Grange. We divert left here, over a stile to follow the footpath, signposted to Hartington. On the other side of the wall there's a concrete dewpond.

6 After 200yds (183m) there's another junction of paths. This time ignore the one signposted to Hartington and keep walking straight on, following the path to Biggin. It stays with the valley round to the right, passing a small sewage works (on the left) before climbing out of the dale to reach the road at Dale End.

WHAT TO LOOK FOR

In Biggin Dale, besides the rampantly prickly gorse bushes, you should see many limestone-loving plants including the purple-flowered meadow cranesbill, patches of delicate harebells, early purple orchids with their dark-spotted stems and leaves, and cheerful orangey-yellow cowslips.

7 Turn right along the road for a few paces then left, following a road past the Waterloo Inn and through Biggin village.

8 Continue up the road to the old railway bridge and here join the Tissington Trail. Follow this old trackbed southwards across the pastures of Biggin and Alport moors. After 2 miles (3.2km) you reach the car park at the former Alsop Station.

WHERE TO EAT AND DRINK

The Waterloo Inn at Biggin is an ideal place for a refreshment break before heading back to Alsop. If you're looking for a delicious bar meal at the end of the day, drive a couple of miles (3.2km) south along the A515 to try the Blue Bell at Tissington Gate.

EXTENDING THE WALK

The obvious choice is to leave the main route at Point **4** and continue along the River Dove through into Beresford Dale, then on into Hartington. Leave the village by Highfield Lane and you can rejoin the route at Point **7** to return to the car park at the start of the walk.

Right: Stone-walled pasture in Beresford Dale, Peak District National Park (Walk 39)

Scaling the Heights of Abraham

A steady climb raises you above the hurley burley of Matlock Bath to a more familiar Peakland landscape.

DISTANCE 8 miles (12.9km)   **MINIMUM TIME** 4hrs 30min

ASCENT/GRADIENT 1,200ft (365m) ▲▲▲ **LEVEL OF DIFFICULTY** ✦✦✦

PATHS Narrow woodland paths, field paths and unsurfaced lanes, lots of stiles

LANDSCAPE Fields and wooded hillsides

SUGGESTED MAP OS Explorer OL24 White Peak

START / FINISH Grid reference: SK 297595

DOG FRIENDLINESS Dogs on lead over farmland

PARKING Pay car park at Artists Corner

PUBLIC TOILETS At car park

Between Matlock and Cromford the River Derwent forges its way through a spectacular, thickly wooded limestone gorge. At Matlock Bath it jostles for space with the bustling A6 highway, the railway to Derby and a string of three-storey houses, shops and amusement parlours, built by the Victorians, who flocked here to take in the healing spa waters. On the hillside to the east lies the gaunt castle of Riber, while Alpine-type cable cars glide up the Heights of Abraham, above cliff tops to the west.

The Heights in Quebec

The original Heights of Abraham, which the hillside must have resembled, rise above Quebec and the St Lawrence River in Canada. There, in 1759, British troops under General Wolfe fought a victorious battle with the French under General Montcalm. Both generals were killed and the encounter earned Wolfe, and Quebec, an unenviable place in English place-name folklore, to be joined later by Waterloo and later still, Spion Kop.

Matlock Bath

Matlock Bath doesn't have time to catch its breath: it's Derbyshire's mini-Blackpool. Yet there are peaceful corners, and this fine walk seeks them out. It offers fine views across the Matlock Gorge. Spurning the cable car, it climbs through the woods and out on to the hillside above the town. The Victoria Prospect Tower peeps over the trees. Built by unemployed miners a century ago it's now part of the Heights of Abraham complex.

Above the complex, a little path leads you through delectable woodland. In spring it's heavy with the scent of wild garlic and coloured by a carpet of bluebells. Out of the woods, an attractive hedge-lined unsurfaced lane weaves its way through high pastures, giving distant views of the White Peak plateau, Black Rocks and the cliffs of Crich Stand.

Bonsall

At the end of the lane, there's Bonsall, whose Perpendicular church tower and spire has been beckoning you onwards for some time. In the centre of

Left: River Derwent, Matlock Bath, Peak District National Park (Walk 40)

this old lead mining village is a sloping market square with a 17th-century cross. The Kings Head Inn, built in 1677, overlooks the square, and is said to be haunted.

The lane out of Bonsall takes you to the edge of an area of old mine shafts and modern-day quarries. Here you're diverted into the woods above the Via Gellia, a valley named after Philip Gell who built the road from the quarry to the Cromford Canal.

Those who wish can make a short diversion from the woodland path to see the Arkwright Centre and the canal in Cromford (see Walk 45). The main route swings north, back into the woods of the Derwent Valley, passing the high hamlet of Upperwood, where fleeting views of Matlock appear through the trees.

WALK 40 DIRECTIONS

❶ Cross the A6 and then take St John's Road up the wooded slopes opposite. It passes beneath St John's Chapel to reach the gates of Cliffe House. Take the path on the right signposted 'Heights of Abraham'. The path climbs steeply upwards through the woods before veering left across the fields above Masson Farm.

2 Beyond the farmhouse and with Victoria Prospect Tower directly ahead, the waymarked path swings right and climbs up to the top of the field. Beyond this the footpath threads through hawthorn thickets before passing one of the entrances to the Heights of Abraham complex.

3 Ignore an obvious, engineered path and continue uphill along the perimeter of the complex and then turn left, going over a wall stile. After crossing a wide vehicle track the narrow footpath re-enters woodland.

4 At the far side of the woods, turn right on to a farm track close to Ember Farm. Join a pleasant lane that winds down pastured hillslopes into Bonsall village.

5 Turn left by the church along a lane that becomes unsurfaced when you get beyond Town End Farm. The lane finally comes to an abrupt end by the high fences of a quarry. Turn left here and follow a wide track around the perimeter of the quarry.

6 Where the fence ends, continue down the track, bending sharply right then left along a narrow path through woodland high above the Via Gellia, then take the left fork after about 300 yds (274m).

7 Turn left when you reach the next junction, following the footpath waymarked for the Derwent Valley Walk (DVW). This climbs further up the wooded bank, then turns left, tracing a mossy wall on the right. It rakes across the wooded hillside, passes above Cromford Court, then climbs away past some cave entrances to a lane at Upperwood. Ignore the next DVW sign and continue along the lane between cottages and past the West Lodge entrance to the Heights of Abraham showcave.

8 After 100yds (91m) leave the surfaced road for a stepped path through the woods on the left, signed 'Matlock'. Climb some steps to a high wooden footbridge over the Heights of Abraham approach road, and then continue on the woodland path. You'll pass under the Heights of Abraham cable cars before joining a farm track that has come in from the left.

9 This joins St John's Lane and the outward route at Cliffe House. Retrace your steps to the start.

Ilam and the Compleat Angler

Explore the countryside once walked by Izaak Walton, often regarded as the 'Father of Angling'.

DISTANCE 4.75 miles (7.7km)	**MINIMUM TIME** 2hrs 30min
ASCENT/GRADIENT 607ft (185m) ▲▲▲	**LEVEL OF DIFFICULTY** ✦✦✦
PATHS Metalled roads, parkland, open hillside, meadows and forest tracks, boggy in wet weather	
LANDSCAPE Parkland, woodland and hillside	
SUGGESTED MAP OS Explorer OL24 White Peak	
START / FINISH Grid reference: SK 131507	
DOG FRIENDLINESS Keep on lead near livestock	
PARKING At Ilam Hall (National Trust pay car park)	
PUBLIC TOILETS At Ilam Hall	

The Manifold and Dove rivers join just beyond Ilam near the Izaak Walton Hotel. Both rivers were fished by the 'Father of Angling' and the author of *The Compleat Angler*, or *The Contemplative Man's Recreation*. Since the first edition appeared in 1653 it has never been out of print.

Izaak Walton

Born in Stafford in 1593, Walton moved to London as an apprentice ironmonger, becoming a craftsman and guild member when he was 25 years old. For most of his working life he owned an ironmongers shop in Fleet Street and lived in a house in Chancery Lane. A keen angler he spent much of his spare time fishing on the Thames but it was not until retirement that he was able to devote himself to his hobby completely. 'I have laid aside business, and gone a-fishing.'

Shrewd Operator

The view we have of Walton from his book is of a genial old buffer strolling along river banks in pastoral England. But nothing could be further from the truth. Walton lived during a period of political upheaval and unrest. In 1649 he saw the execution of Charles I and left London for Staffordshire where he stayed during the Civil War. A staunch Royalist he is mentioned amongst the supporters of Charles II after the Battle of Worcester in 1651. Following the battle he visited a friend who had been imprisoned in Stafford. From this friend Walton received the King's ring, which he delivered to Colonel Blague, then a prisoner in the Tower of London. The Colonel escaped, made his way to France and returned the ring to the King. If Walton had been caught, he would have been executed. Just two years after 'the only known adventure' in his life he published his famous book.

Celebrated Work

The Compleat Angler is the story of three sportsmen, Viator, a huntsman, Auceps, a fowler and Piscator, the fisherman, walking the River Lea on

ILAM

May Day debating the finer points of their chosen sport. The fifth edition in 1676 contained an addition by Walton's friend and fishing companion, Charles Cotton, who lived at Beresford Hall near Hartington. Cotton built a little fishing house on the banks of the Dove near his home, which still stands today. This 'holy shrine for all anglers' has the interlacing initials of both men and the inscription 'Piscatoribus Scarum 1674'.

Following the restoration of the monarchy and Charles II, Walton moved to Winchester as the guest of his friend George Morley, Bishop of Winchester, and lived there until he died, aged 90 on 15 December 1683. He was buried in the floor of the Chapel of St John the Evangelist and the Fisherman Apostles.

WALK 41 DIRECTIONS

❶ Leave the car park from the corner (pedestrian exit), turn right through a gate and follow the track through the park. Cross a stile and turn left on to the road out of Ilam village. Go uphill, turn left at Park Cottage on to the Castern to Throwley road. At a Y-junction go left, following the road across Rushley Bridge.

❷ Go through Rushley Farm and then turn right, through a gate, on to the public footpath. Cross a ladder stile, walk along the side of a fence and then cross a gate on the left. Continue ahead following the waymarked path beside a stone wall and a fence, walking along the valley bottom.

3 Go over a series of stiles and at the final one, turn left on to the road. At the crossroads turn left towards Ashbourne. Go left through a gap stile at the next public footpath sign and cross the field. Cross a stile, go through another field to a stile to the left of a farm, then head diagonally left across the next field.

4 Cross the wall by stone steps, head diagonally right to a gap stile to the right of some buildings. Continue on this line to another stile in the hedge to the right of Fieldhead farm and turn left on to the road. Follow this round the boundary of the farm and go over a stile on the right by a metal gate.

5 Follow the field-edge path uphill. Cross a stile, cross the field to where two walls meet at a corner and follow the wall to the right. Join a farm road, pass a derelict farmstead, then turn diagonally right across a field and through a gap stile in the wall at the far corner.

6 Follow the direction pointer past two marker stones to the next public footpath sign and go right. Follow the wall on your right, go through a gap, follow the waymarker downhill.

7 Go across two fields, a stile and then a bridge and into Ilam Park. Turn right and at the stile fork left, uphill, on a broad track that crosses the grounds back to the car park.

Dovedale: Ivory Spires and Wooded Splendour

*A walk through the alpine-like splendour
of the Peak's most famous dale.*

DISTANCE *5 miles (8km)* **MINIMUM TIME** *3hrs 30min*

ASCENT/GRADIENT *557ft (170m)* ▲▲▲ **LEVEL OF DIFFICULTY** +++

PATHS *Mostly good paths, lanes, a few stiles, one small scramble*

LANDSCAPE *Partially wooded dales and high pastures*

SUGGESTED MAP *OS Explorer OL24 White Peak*

START / FINISH *Grid reference: SK 146509*

DOG FRIENDLINESS *Dogs should be kept under close control*

PARKING *Dovedale pay car park, near Thorpe*

PUBLIC TOILETS *At car park*

Right from the start there's drama as you follow the River Dove, wriggling through a narrow gorge between Bunster Hill and the towering pyramid of Thorpe Cloud. A limestone path urges you to climb to a bold rocky outcrop high above the river. Lovers' Leap has a fine view across the dale to pinnacles of the Twelve Apostles. It's a view to gladden your hearts – not the sort of place you'd think of throwing yourself from at all. However, in 1761 an Irish dean and his lady companion, who were out horse riding (or were they horsing about?) fell off the rock. The dean died of his injuries but the lady survived to tell the tale.

Spires and Caves

The Dove writhes round another corner. Above your heads, flaky fingers of limestone known as the Tissington Spires rise out from thick woodland cover. Just a few footsteps away on the right there's a splendid natural arch, which is just outside the entrance to Reynard's Cave. This is the result of the cave's roof collapsing.

The dale's limestone walls close in. The path climbs to a place more remote from the rushing river, which often floods around here. As the valley opens out again two gigantic rock stacks face each other across the Dove. Pickering Tor has a small cave at its foot. A little footbridge allows you across to the other side to the foot of Ilam Rock. This 80ft (25m) leaning thumb of limestone has an overhang on the south side that's popular with climbers. It too has a cave at the bottom, which is only 4ft (1.2m) at the entrance but opens out to over 30ft (10m) inside.

You will get a better view of them when you cross the little footbridge to the cave at the foot of the rocks. On this side you're in Staffordshire and the paths are less populated.

Hurt's Wood and Hall Dale

The continuing walk into Hall Dale heralds a less formal landscape. The dale is dry and it climbs up the hillside. Hurts Wood has wych elm, whitebeam, ash and rowan. Some fences have kept grazing animals out, allowing the trees and shrubs to regenerate. Hurts Wood is alive and well. You'll hear and see many birds — warblers, redstarts and black caps; and you'll see wild flowers — dog's mercury, wood anemone and wood forget-me-not.

It seems a shame to leave the dale behind but soon you're walking down a quiet lane with Ilam and the beautiful Manifold Valley on your right and a shapely peak, Bunster Hill, on your left. A path takes you across the shoulder of the hill, across the ridge and furrow of a medieval field system, then back into the valley of the Dove.

WALK 42 DIRECTIONS

❶ Turn right out of the car park and follow the road along the west bank of the Dove. Cross the footbridge to the opposite bank and turn left along a wide footpath. This twists and turns through the narrow dale, between Bunster Hill and Thorpe Cloud.

❷ Follow the path as it climbs some steps up through the woods on to the famous rocky outcrop of Lovers' Leap, then descends past the magnificent Tissington Spires and Reynard's Cave. Here a huge natural arch surrounds the much smaller entrance to the historic cave. As the dale narrows the path climbs above the river.

3 The dale widens again. Leave the main path for a route signposted 'Public Footpath to Stanshope', and cross the footbridge over the Dove. A narrow woodland path turns right beneath the huge spire of Ilam Rock above you. Ignore the path on the left, signposted to Ilam '(steep ascent)'. Beyond a stile the path eases to the left into Hall Dale. Following the valley bottom, as it climbs out of the woods into a rugged limestone-cragged gorge.

4 As the gorge begins to become shallow the path enters pastureland – the attractive village of Stanshope is now on the skyline. At a crossroads of paths turn left through a squeeze stile in the wall and head south with a stone wall on the right. Where the wall turns right, keep walking straight ahead to reach another stile, and then veer half right by a wall in the next field. The path cuts diagonally to the left across the last two fields to reach Ilam-Moor Lane, 250yds (229m) to the south of Damgate Farm.

5 Turn left to walk along the lovely quiet country lane. There are magnificent views from here down to Ilam and the Manifold Valley ahead of you and down to the right.

6 After 800yds (732m) take a footpath on the left, following the drive to Ilamtops Farm for a few paces before turning right over a stile. A field path now heads

roughly south-east, traversing low grassy fellsides to the top of Moor Plantation woods.

7 Here the path (fallen away in places) cuts across the steep sides of Bunster Hill, before straddling its south spur and descending to a step-stile in the intake wall. A clear path now descends south-east across sloping pastures to the back of the Izaak Walton Hotel.

8 Turn left (north-east) by the hotel across more fields and back to the car park.

EXTENDING THE WALK

As so often when walking beside the River Dove, it's difficult to resist the temptation to carry on following its lovely series of dales. You can do this at Point **A**, continuing up the dale to Viator's Bridge, a packhorse bridge in lovely Milldale, before heading back across the fields to rejoin the main route at Point **B**. The bridge on the route takes its name from a character in Izaak Walton's *Compleat Angler,* who complains to his companion Piscator that the bridge is too small – 'Why a mouse can hardly go over it: 'Tis not two fingers broad.'

A Tissington Trail of Two Villages

Joining the famous trackbed Tissington Trail between the differing villages of Parwich and Tissington.

DISTANCE *4.25 miles (6.8km)*   **MINIMUM TIME** *2hrs 30min*

ASCENT/GRADIENT *525ft (160m)* ▲▲▲   **LEVEL OF DIFFICULTY** +++

PATHS *Field paths, lanes and an old railway trackbed, lots of stiles*

LANDSCAPE *Village and rolling farm pastures*

SUGGESTED MAP *OS Explorer OL24 White Peak*

START / FINISH *Grid reference: SK 177522*

DOG FRIENDLINESS *Mostly on farmland, keep dogs on lead*

PARKING *Tissington Trail pay car park*

PUBLIC TOILETS *At car park*

The approach to Tissington is through a magnificent avenue of lime trees, and when you first see the place it completes the idyll of a perfect village. On one side of a huge green is Tissington Hall, the home of the Fitzherbert family since the reign of Elizabeth I; on the other a neat row of cottages and a slightly elevated Norman church. The trouble with Tissington is that it is too perfect, and to avoid the crowds you'll have to visit mid-week.

On this walk you save Tissington village for last, preferring instead to take to the Tissington Trail, the former trackbed of the Ashbourne-to-Buxton railway, which was closed by Dr Beeching in 1967. The route soon leaves the old track behind and descends into the valley of Bletch Brook, then out again on to a pastured hillside. Now you see Parwich, tucked in the next valley beneath a wooded hill. Overlooking the village is a fine 18th-century red-bricked building, Parwich Hall.

Parwich

Parwich isn't as grand as Tissington, but it has a village green, and there's a duck pond too. You may see moorhens and their young swimming about among the tangled irises. But Parwich is a more peaceful place and the winding lanes are almost traffic-free in comparison. St Peter's Church is Victorian, but incorporates the chancel arch, and a carved tympanum from the old Norman church.

Leaving Parwich behind, the path continues over the hillside, back into the valley of Bletch Brook and the Tissington Trail, then back for a better look at Tissington. If you go round the lane clockwise you will pass the Methodist chapel before coming to one of Tissington's five wells, the Coffin Well. Every year on Ascension Day Tissington's locals dress these wells. This involves making a clay-covered dressing frame on to which pictures are traced. Flower petals are then pressed into the clay, creating the elaborate patterns and pictures you see. The ceremony is unique to Derbyshire and the Peak District. Originally a pagan ceremony to appease the gods into keeping pure water flowing, it was later adopted by the Christian religion.

TISSINGTON

During the Black Death, when people from neighbouring villages were being ravaged by the plague, the Tissington villagers were kept in good health, due, they believe, to the pure water from the five wells. Just past the Coffin Well there's a fine duck pond, complete with a handful of ever-hungry ducks, but most eyes will be on the magnificent Jacobean hall. If it's closed to visitors, you can view it through the fine wrought-iron gates built by Robert Bakewell, or get an elevated view from the churchyard.

WALK 43 DIRECTIONS

❶ From the Tissington Trail car park follow the trackbed of the north-east bound Tissington Trail, (the former Ashbourne-to-Buxton railway). After about 800yds (732m) leave the trail by a path on the left that crosses right, over a bridge and along a cart track.

❷ Just past the first bend descend on the waymarked but trackless path into the valley of Bletch Brook, going through several stiles at the field boundaries and across a footbridge spanning the brook itself. A more definite path establishes itself on the climb out of the valley. It reaches the top of a pastured spur, well to the right of a small cottage.

3 In the next high field the path follows a hedge on the left to a stile in the field corner. It then descends to a footpath signpost, which points the short way across the last field to the western edge of the village.

4 For those who want to explore the village turn right, otherwise turn left down the lane to Brook Close Farm. A signposted footpath on the left shows the slanting route up across the pasture. The path now heads south-westwards to the top right-hand corner of the field, then follows a muddy tree-lined track for a few paces.

WHILE YOU'RE THERE

Tissington Hall has been home to he Fitzherbert family for the best part of 400 years, built by Francis Fitzherbert in 1609 to replace a moated manor house. There are public tours in July and August. Visit www.tissington-hall.com for up-to-date details.

5 On entering the next field turn left. Follow a hedge on the left, then descends to recross Bletch Brook via a footbridge (not the concrete farm bridge to the left). It climbs up the middle of the next long field before zig-zagging up the steep upper slopes to reach the bridge over the Tissington

WHAT TO LOOK OUT FOR

Many of the regularly ploughed fields of Parwich and Tissington will have a few wild flowers in them, but take a look at the field-edges and the hayfields, for they will be rich in limestone-loving plants. In April and May, keep a watch for the increasingly rare cowslip (*Primula veris*). Its short single stem grows from a rosette of wrinkled leaves and its yellow flowers form a drooping cluster.

WHERE TO EAT AND DRINK

The Old Coach House tea rooms at Tissington serves coffee, lunch and afternoon teas 11am–5pm. The Sycamore Inn in Parwich looks a little plain from the outside but serves good bar meals. The Bluebell Inn near the exit gates of the Tissington Estate has a good reputation for bar meals and an extensive menu.

Trail. Go down to the trail and follow it north-westwards (right) along an embankment through the Crakelow cutting.

6 After about 500yds (457m) turn left, following the Tissington footpath over a stile to the right-hand corner of a field. Now follow a wall on the right, all the way down to the road at the edge of Tissington village.

7 Maintain your direction along the lane to reach Chapel Lane. You can walk either way round the village square. The hall and church are straight ahead, while the Methodist chapel and the Coffin Well are on Chapel Lane to the left. The car park lies to the south-east of the square; take a left turn just beyond the Coffin Well.

EXTENDING THE WALK

Leaving Parwich it's possible to extend this walk to another local village – Alsop en le Dale. From Point **5** pick out a field path route which eventually comes to the lane leading into Alsop en le Dale. Walk through the village and find a path on the far side which brings you to Stonepit Plantation and a car park on the Tissington Trail. You can follow the trail all the way back to Tissington, or turn off right at Newton Grange to emerge on the edge of the village by Point **7**.

Skeletons from the Past

Miners' tracks to the lead village of Brassington.

DISTANCE *5.5 miles (8.8km)*   MINIMUM TIME *3hrs 30min*

ASCENT/GRADIENT *1,148ft (350m)* ▲▲▲ LEVEL OF DIFFICULTY +++

PATHS *Hill paths, some hard to follow, and railway trackbed, numerous stiles*

LANDSCAPE *Limestone hills*

SUGGESTED MAP *OS Explorer OL24 White Peak*

START / FINISH *Grid reference: SK 249528*

DOG FRIENDLINESS *Dogs on leads over farmland, can run free on long stretches of enclosed railway trackbed*

PARKING *Sheepwash pay car park by Carsington Reservoir*

PUBLIC TOILETS *None on route*

He was as lean as a skeleton, pale as a dead corpse, his hair and beard a deep black, his flesh lank, and, as we thought, something of the colour of lead itself.

So wrote Daniel Defoe on seeing a lead miner, who had been living in a cave at Harborough Rocks. In times past Carsington and Brassington lived and breathed lead. Prior to the construction of Carsington Reservoir, archaeologists discovered a Romano-British settlement here, which could have been the long-lost *Ludutarum*, the centre of the lead-mining industry in Roman times.

As you walk out of Carsington into the world of the miner, you're using the very tracks he would have used. But the lesions and pockmarks of the endless excavations are being slowly healed by time, and many wild flowers are beginning to proliferate in the meadows and on hillsides.

Brassington

Weird-shaped limestone crags top the hill, then Brassington appears in the next valley with its Norman church tower rising above the grey rooftops of its 17th- and 18th-century houses. Brassington's former post office used to be the tollhouse for the Loughborough turnpike. St James Church is largely Norman, though it was heavily restored in the late 19th century, including the north aisle, which was added in 1880. The impressive south arcade has fine Perpendicular windows. High on the inner walls of the Norman tower is a figure of a man with his hand on his heart. The carving is believed to be Saxon: the man, Brassington's oldest resident.

Climbing out of Brassington the route takes you over Hipley Hill, where there are more remnants of the mines, and more limestone outcrops. On the top you could have caught the train back, but the Cromford High Peak railway closed in 1967, so you are left with a walk along its trackbed. It's a pleasant walk though, through a wooded cutting, with meadow cranesbill and herb Robert thriving among trackside verges and crags.

153

CARSINGTON RESERVOIR

Harborough Rocks beckon from the left. Archaeologists have uncovered evidence that sabre-toothed tigers, black bears and hyenas once sought the shelter of nearby caves. They also discovered relics and artefacts from Roman and Iron-Age dwellers. For those with extra time, there's an entertaining path winding between the popular climbing crags to the summit, which gives wide views across the White Peak and the lowlands of the East Midlands. Carsington Reservoir is seen to perfection, surrounded by chequered fields, woods and low rounded hills. Leaving the railway behind, there's one last hill, Carsington Pasture, to descend before returning to the lake.

WALK 44 DIRECTIONS

❶ Take the signposted path northwards towards Carsington. It winds through scrub woods and rounds a finger of the lake before reaching the B5035 road.

The path continues on the other side, meeting a lane by Wash Farm and going straight on to enter the village by the Miners Arms.

❷ Turn left along the lane to reach the Hopton road. Where

the road turns left go straight ahead along a narrow lane passing several cottages. Beyond a gate the lane becomes a fine green track beneath the limestone-studded slopes of Carsington Pasture.

3 Where the track swings left you reach a gate; go through the gate then immediately fork right off the main path on a path climbing the grassy slopes to the west. At the top aim right of a copse and go through a gap in the broken wall before descending into a little valley.

4 Go over two stiles to cross a green lane, then follow a miners' track for 200yds (183m) towards

WHERE TO EAT AND DRINK

You can break the route for refreshment at Ye Old Gate Inn in Brassington, which serves Marstons ales. Children must be ten years old or over.

some old mine workings. Here a footpath sign directs you around some limestone outcrops before arcing right towards Brassington. Turn left at the wall stile and follow the waymarked route across the fields into the village.

5 Turn left, then immediately right up Miners Hill. Now go right up Jasper Lane, left up Red Lion Hill, and left again along Hillside Lane. After 200yds (183m) leave the lane for a

WHAT TO LOOK OUT FOR

Despite their apparently sterile soil, the spoil tips have been colonised by a range of lead-tolerant plants, flourishing among the grassy heaps. You may see mountain pansy, spring sandwort, eyebright or autumn gentians.

WHILE YOU'RE THERE

Take a look round Hognaston, an ancient Norse settlement dominated by its fine church dedicated to St Bartholomew. The church dates back to 1200 and has an ornate Norman doorway with a tympanium showing a bishop and his crook, with lambs and wild beasts. In medieval times the church tower with its 5-ft (1.5m) thick walls was used as a defensive keep to protect the villagers' livestock.

footpath on the right, which climbs past more limestone outcrops. The faint path gradually veers right, and passes the head of a green lane.

6 Here climb right over the pathless wall stile. Through the next three fields the path climbs parallel to, and to the right of, a line of wooden electricity pylons. In the fourth field bear half right above the rock outcrops and go through the top gate. Now aim for the extensive buildings of Longcliffe Dale Farm. After going over the next stile, turn left up the road, passing the farm. A footpath on the right then cuts a corner to the High Peak Trail, passing an electricity substation and Peak Quarry Farm.

7 Turn right along the trackbed of the High Peak Trail passing the Harborough Rocks.

8 Go right at the footpath signed to Carsington. This descends a small field to cross Manystones Lane. Follow the wall across Carsington Pasture, then descend by woods to a gate by a cottage.

9 Turn left down a little ginnel leading to the road and left again to retrace your earlier route back to Sheepwash car park.

Overleaf: View over Cromford from Black Rocks, Peak District National Park (Walk 45)

Cromford and the Black Rocks

Walk through the Industrial Revolution in a valley where history was made.

WALK 45

DISTANCE 5 miles (8km)	**MINIMUM TIME** 3hrs
ASCENT/GRADIENT 720ft (220m) ▲▲▲	**LEVEL OF DIFFICULTY** ✦✦✦

PATHS Well-graded – canal tow paths, lanes, forest paths and a railway trackbed, quite a few stiles

LANDSCAPE Town streets and wooded hillsides

SUGGESTED MAP OS Explorer OL24 White Peak

START / FINISH Grid reference: SK 300571

DOG FRIENDLINESS Dogs on lead over farmland, can run free on long stretches of enclosed railway trackbed

PARKING Cromford Wharf pay car park

PUBLIC TOILETS At car park

For many centuries Cromford, 'the ford by the bend in the river', was no more than a sleepy backwater. Lead mining brought the village brief prosperity, but by the 18th century even that was in decline. Everything changed in 1771 when Sir Richard Arkwright decided to build the world's first water-powered cotton-spinning mill here. Within 20 years he had built two more, and had constructed a whole new town around them. Cromford was awake to the Industrial Revolution and would be connected to the rest of Britain by a network of roads, railways and canals.

As you walk through the cobbled courtyard of the Arkwright Mill, now being restored by the Arkwright Society, you are transported back into that austere world of the 18th century, back to the times when mother, father and children all worked at the mills.

Most of the town actually lies on the other side of the traffic-laden A6, including the mill pond which was built by Arkwright to impound the waters of Bonsall Brook, and the beautifully restored mill workers' cottages of North Street.

The Black Rocks

The Black Rocks overlook the town from the south. The walk makes a beeline for them through little ginnels, past some almshouses and through pine woods. You'll see climbers grappling with the 80ft (24m) gritstone crags, but there's a good path all the way to the top. Here you can look across the Derwent Valley to the gaunt skeleton of Riber Castle, to the beacon on top of Crich Stand and down the Derwent Gorge to Matlock.

The Cromford and High Peak Railway

The next stage of the journey takes you on to the High Peak Trail, which uses the former trackbed of the Cromford and High Peak Railway. Engineered by Josias Jessop and constructed in the 1830s, the railway was built as an extension of the canal system and, as such, the stations were called wharfs.

CROMFORD

In the early years horses pulled the wagons on the level stretches, while steam-winding engines worked the inclines. By the mid-1800s steam engines worked the whole line, which connected with the newly extended Midland Railway. The railway was closed by Dr Beeching in 1967.

The Canal

After abandoning the High Peak Trail pleasant forest paths lead you down into the valley at High Peak Junction, where the old railway met the Cromford Canal. The 33-mile (53.5km) canal was built in 1793, a year after Arkwright's death, to link up with the Erewash, thus completing a navigable waterway to the River Trent at Trent Lock. Today, there's an information centre here, a fascinating place to muse before that final sojourn along the tow path to Cromford.

WALK 45 DIRECTIONS

❶ Turn left out of the car park on to Mill Road. Cross the A6 to the Market Place. Turn right down Scarthin, passing the Boat Inn and the old millpond before doubling back left along Water Lane to Cromford Hill.

❷ Turn right, past the shops and Bell Inn, then turn left up

Bedehouse Lane, which turns into a narrow tarmac ginnel and heads upgill past some almshouses (otherwise known as bedehouses).

3 At the top of the lane by a street of 1970s housing, a signpost for Black Rocks points uphill. The footpath continues its climb southwards to meet a lane. Turn left along the winding lane, which soon divides. Take the right fork, a surfaced track leading to a stone-built house with woods behind. On reaching the house, turn right through a gate, and then follow the top field edge.

4 After climbing some steps, ascend left through the woods of Dimons Dale up to the Black Rocks car park and picnic site. The track you've reached is on the former trackbed of the Cromford and High Peak Railway. Immediately opposite is the there-and-back waymarked detour leading to the rocks.

5 Returning to the car park, turn right along the High Peak Trail, which traverses the hillside high above Cromford.

6 After 0.75 mile (1.2km) take a path on the right off the incline for Intake Lane. At the lane, turn right and follow it to a sharp right-hand bend. Here, go straight on, following a path heading south-east along the top edge of some woodland. (Please note that neither the path nor the

WHAT TO LOOK OUT FOR

Besides the Arkwright Mill, which is a 'must see', take some time to visit the exhibits in old railway workshops at Highpeak Junction and the Leawood Pumping Station, which pumped water from the River Derwent to the Cromford Canal. The restored Leawood works has a working Cornish-type beam engine.

wood is shown on the current OS Explorer OL24 White Peak.)

7 On nearing Birchwood Farm, watch out for two paths coming up from the left. Take the second smaller one descending more directly downhill in a sunken channel. At the bottom of the woods the path swings left across a field, coming out to the A6 road by Oak Farm.

8 Cross the road and follow the little ginnel opposite, over the Cromford Canal by the Highpeak Junction information centre. Turn left before the Matlock Railway and along the canal tow path. Follow this back to the car park at Cromford Wharf.

WHERE TO EAT AND DRINK

Arkwright's Mill has a café for coffee, cake and light snacks. The excellent Boat Inn free house on Scarthin at Cromford serves bar meals at lunchtimes and evenings and has a beer garden.

WHILE YOU'RE THERE

If you have time, visit Wirksworth, a former lead-mining town on the hillsides above Cromford. Until a restoration project of the 1980s Wirksworth had become a dusty, derelict place that nobody wanted to visit. Take a look at the National Stone Centre on Portway Lane. Here you can have a go at gem panning and join guided walks. The Wirksworth Heritage Centre, which is housed in a former silk and velvet mill at Crown Yard, gives a fascinating insight into the town's history.

Climbing up to Crich in Search of Cardale

On Crich Chase through TV-land to the monument of Crich Stand.

DISTANCE *7.5 miles (12.1km)* MINIMUM TIME *5hrs*

ASCENT/GRADIENT *721ft (220m)* ▲▲▲ LEVEL OF DIFFICULTY +++

PATHS *Woodland and field paths and canal tow path, many stiles*

LANDSCAPE *Woods and pastured hills*

SUGGESTED MAP *OS Explorer OL24 White Peak*

START / FINISH *Grid reference: SK 349517*

DOG FRIENDLINESS *Keep on lead across farmland, also by canal to protect the wildlife of nature reserve*

PARKING *Ambergate, car park by station*

PUBLIC TOILETS *At A6/A610 junction at start and at Crich near Black Swan*

The first five minutes of the walk are as uneventful as the rest is fascinating, and include such delights as a modern railway station and a busy road with heavy traffic. But as soon as you've turned the corner and crossed over Chase Bridge you're walking in a different world. An ivy-clad wall effectively blocks sight and sound of the road, the railway and the canal, tangled with irises and pondweed ,ambles by slowly through the trees. Watch out for the bright yellow-and-black spotted longhorn beetle feeding on the meadowsweet and the holly blue butterflies in springtime.

Familiar to Millions

On this journey you save the greater part of the canal walking to the end, in order to climb through the woodland of Crich Chase, once part of a hunting forest owned by the 13th-century Norman baron, Hubert FitzRalph. After climbing high fields and along a gritstone edge, known as the Tors, you come upon Crich (pronounced so the 'i' rhymes with eye). If you get that déjà-vu feeling it's because Crich was *Peak Practice's* Cardale until the series moved to Longnor (see Walk 31) in 2001. Past the market cross and across more fields you come to the National Tramway Museum, which is well worth a visit.

But you can't stay all day: there is a walk to be done! It continues to its high point on Crich Stand, a limestone crag isolated by an area of gritstone. Capping the Stand is a 60ft (19m) beacon tower, rebuilt in 1921 to commemorate the Sherwood Foresters killed in the two World Wars. On a clear day you can pick out Lincoln and its cathedral. Often you'll see kestrels hovering around the cliff edge, searching for their prey.

The path descends through more woodland, beneath the shady gritstone cliffs of the old Dukes Quarry and down to the canal at Whatstandwell. The canal here has been allowed to silt up, and has become a haven for wildlife. It's well known for its many varieties of hoverfly, its azure damselflies and brown chinamark moths.

WALK 46

Wealth of Wildlife

Yellow irises and flowering rush, which has pink flowers, can be seen on the water's edge, while broad-leaved pondweed clogs the middle of the canal. That doesn't seem to impede the moorhens or mallards though. By the time you get back to Ambergate you will have seen a wealth of wildlife, but you can rest assured that much more wildlife will have seen you.

WALK 46 DIRECTIONS

❶ Leave the car park at Ambergate Station and walk down the road under the bridge and then turn right along the busy A6. Turn right up Chase Road, which cuts underneath the railway bridge to the Cromford Canal. Follow the tow path northwards to the next bridge.

❷ Go over the bridge before following a footpath climbing into the woodland of Crich Chase. In the upper reaches of the wood the waymarked path swings left; follow it to pass through some small clearings. It then follows a wall on the right at the top edge of the wood. Turn right over a stile, then climb across two fields to reach Chadwick Nick Lane.

CRICH

❸ Turn right along the road. After 300yds (274m) a path on the left begins with some steps and a stile, and continues the climb northwards across numerous fields with stiles and gates – and by the rock outcrops of The Tors.

❹ The path becomes an enclosed ginnel, which emerges on Sandy Lane. Follow this to the Market Square, where you turn left, then right along Coasthill. Coasthill leads to an unsurfaced lane. Where the lane ends, follow a path in the same direction across fields to join another lane by some houses. Follow this to Carr Lane, then turn right, passing the entrance to the National Tramway Museum.

❺ Continue along the road to a sharp right-hand bend, then turn left along the approach road to Crich Stand, topped by the Sherwood Foresters Monument. There's a small fee if you want to go up to the viewing platform on the monument, but otherwise continue along the public right of way on the right. The footpath, signed to Wakebridge and Plaistow, veers half right through shrubs and bramble, before circumnavigating Cliff Quarry.

❻ The path then crosses over the museum's tram track near its terminus, before winding down the hillside through attractive scrub woodland. It joins a wide track that descends past Wakebridge and Cliff farms before coming to a road.

WHAT TO LOOK OUT FOR

St Mary's Church was consecrated in 1135. It has a Perpendicular spired west tower with a Norman north arcade and a 14th-century chancel. Inside there is a circular Norman font, which is unusually large, and many tombs, including the one of Sir William de Wakebridge, whose family were wiped out by the plague.

❼ Turn right along the road for a few paces, then turn left on a footpath. This descends south across fields before swinging right to enter a wood. A well-defined path passes beneath quarried rockfaces, and crosses a minor road before reaching the canal at Whatstandwell.

❽ Turn left and follow a most delightful tow path for 2 miles (3.2km) through the shade of tree boughs. At Chase Bridge you meet the outward route and retrace your steps back to the car park.

WHERE TO EAT AND DRINK

The Hurt Arms at Ambergate is a popular family-friendly pub that serves food daily, but for those with more sophisticated tastes, try the Black Swan by the Market Place in Crich.

WALK 47

Strutting the Ancient Tracks of Beaurepaire

A pleasing ramble around Belper and the surrounding countryside, once a Norman hunting ground.

DISTANCE *5 miles (8km)*   MINIMUM TIME *3hrs 30min*

ASCENT/GRADIENT *590ft (180m)* ▲▲▲   LEVEL OF DIFFICULTY ✛✛✛

PATHS *Good paths and track, could be muddy after periods of heavy rain, quite a few stiles*

LANDSCAPE *Urban start and finish, but mostly rolling farm pastures*

SUGGESTED MAP *OS Explorer 259 Derby*

START / FINISH *Grid reference: SK 346481*

DOG FRIENDLINESS *Dogs should be kept on lead through farmland*

PARKING *Derwent Valley Visitor Centre, North Mill, Belper*

PUBLIC TOILETS *Nearby Bridge Street*

Before Jedediah Strutt came to Belper, it was just a mere backwater of Derbyshire, and according to Dr Davies, writing in 1811 was 'backward in civility' and considered as the insignificant residence of a few 'uncivilised nailors'. The land around Belper was part of the Norman hunting grounds of Beaurepaire, which meant beautiful retreat. The land was first handed to Henri de Ferrieres and the family ruled here until 1266, when Henry III handed them over to his son the Earl of Leicester, known as Edmund Crouchback.

Strutt's Legacy

Jedediah Strutt had earlier partnered Richard Arkwright in the building of the world's first water-powered cotton mill, sited upriver at Cromford (see Walk 45). The success of that project prompted him to build the South Mill, here at Belper. By 1786 he had built the timber-framed North Mill. Jedediah died in 1797 but his three sons, William, George and Joseph built on his successes. In 30 years there were five mills in the town, though the original North Mill had to be replaced in 1803 after a damaging fire. The Strutts took an active interest in the welfare of their community, providing good housing for their workforce and schooling for the children. As you walk past the North Mill you can see a bridge connecting it with the mill across the road. Note the gun loopholes in it. They were to protect the mills from Luddites, but fortunately the expected trouble never materialised.

Rural Scenes

Most of the walk is rural, and you're soon tramping through woods and across fields. The small lake you see is now a nature reserve, well known for wildfowl. Farm tracks that wouldn't look out of place in a Gainsborough or Constable landscape take you up the hillside to Belper Lane End.

At the top of the hill you reach Longwalls Lane, which was part of the Saxon Portway road. Archaeological finds show that the lane was in use, not only by the Romans, but prehistoric man. In such times the ridges made safer routes than the swampy forests of the valleys, with their dangerous wild animals. The old highway starts unpromisingly as a tarmac lane, but soon becomes a splendid thicket-lined track, with oak trees, wild flowers and wide views up the Derwent Valley. The monument-topped cliff in the distance is Crich Stand (see Walk 46).

Coming down to Blackbrook the route discovers a delightful woodland track above Lumb Brook. Known locally as Depth o' Lumb the wood is coloured by great swathes of bluebells in spring and Himalayan balsam in summer. After descending the slopes of Chevin Mount, the route returns to Belper by the banks of the Derwent, the river that supplied the power for Derbyshire's role in the Industrial Revolution.

WALK 47 DIRECTIONS

1 From the car park at the visitor centre, turn right on to Belper Bridge over the River Derwent. Cross over the bridge then, when you reach the

Talbot Hotel, take the right fork following the signpost for 'Belper Lane End and Alderwasley'.

2 Ignore the next right fork, Wyver Lane, but where the road swings sharply left, go straight ahead on a short, unsurfaced lane, called The Scotches. Continue over a stile at the end of the lane for a cross-field path. It finally descends through woodland to reach Wyver Lane opposite a wetlands nature reserve.

3 Turn left along the road for a few paces, then left again on a bridleway track, which arcs left to pass straight through the yard of Wyver Farm before continuing to the road at Belper Lane End.

4 Turn right along the road, passing the Bull's Head pub and then take the left fork to Gorses Farm. Here a farm track climbs past some chicken sheds before reaching a T-junction of country lanes.

5 Turn left along Longwalls Lane, which soon degenerates into a stony track. Continue to follow the track downhill and keep straight ahead along a less well-defined track. In time this becomes a walled path before returning to a proper lane again beyond a large house. The lane then meets Ashbourne Road at Blackbrook.

6 Turn right along the road for about 200yds (183m), then turn left over a footbridge by a ford. Follow the lane for 600yds (549m) to a footpath on the left, highlighted by Midshires Way waymarkers. Go through the squeeze stile and follow the well-defined field path climbing to the south-east. The path enters an area

of delightful woodland through Lumb Grange, then turns left at a stile in a wall, aiming for some houses at the far end of a field. Take the right-hand of two parallel tracks, past the houses to reach the road at Farnah Green.

7 Turn right along the road to walk through the village. After 150yds (137m) follow the Midshires Way along an unsurfaced lane by Chevin Mount. Just beyond the sharp right-hand bend in the lane turn left along a footpath. This descends directly through sloping fields eastwards to Chevin Road.

8 The continuing path is staggered 200yds (183m) to the north and follows a short driveway to the stile at the end. Beyond this go left on a clear footpath across fields and down to the River Derwent. Follow the various riverside paths and tracks back to Belper Bridge and the outward route.

Among Aristocracy at Osmaston and Shirley Parks

Two estates provide gentle parkland walking.

DISTANCE 4.5 miles (7.2km)	**MINIMUM TIME** 3hrs 30min

DISTANCE 4.5 miles (7.2km)   **MINIMUM TIME** 3hrs 30min
ASCENT/GRADIENT 295ft (90m) ▲▲▲   **LEVEL OF DIFFICULTY** ✦✦✦
PATHS Estate tracks and field paths, quite a few stiles
LANDSCAPE Park, woodland and farm pasture
SUGGESTED MAP OS Explorer 259 Derby
START / FINISH Grid reference: SK 200435
DOG FRIENDLINESS Dogs should be on lead
PARKING Osmaston village hall car park
PUBLIC TOILETS None on route

Osmaston is barely a few winding country lanes away from the buzzing traffic of Ashbourne, but it's just the unspoiled tranquil village you'd hope to find on a country walk. The moment you leave the car you will experience the slow tick-over of the place.

Mock Tudor

St Martin's Church was built in 1845 to replace a much earlier one. The parish register goes back to 1606. It's full of references to the Wright family, who for a long time were the local gentry and benefactors to the village. Francis Wright, the owner of the Butterley Iron Works, had Osmaston Hall built here in 1849. The hall itself was a mock-Tudor mansion and the gardens were landscaped. There's a memorial to him found in Ashbourne's Market Place.

In 1964 the hall's owner, Sir John Walker, decided to demolish the place when he moved to Okeover and took the Okeover family name. However the grounds, Osmaston Park, are criss-crossed by rights of way, and make a pleasing itinerary for the walker.

Across the road from the car park is a terrace of four thatched cottages, built to celebrate the coronation of King George VI. As you walk down the lane you pass the Shoulder of Mutton, a fine village pub with much promise for the end of the day, then some more of those thatched cottages, this time built with rustic tawny-coloured local bricks. These cottages are much older than the ones seen earlier and they're timber framed.

At the end of the lane there's a duck pond. Even the ducks seem less noisy in Osmaston. The walk enters the woodlands of Osmaston Park and threads between two of the estate's many lakes. On the other side there's an old mill, built in the style of an Austrian chalet and complete with a waterwheel. The path climbs though more woodland.

Shirley's another pretty village with its own aristocracy – Earl Ferrers and the Shirley family. Viscount Tamworth, the heir to Earl Ferrers, still

WALK 48

lives in the village. From Shirley the walk turns back across fields and woods to Osmaston Park, reaching another of the estate's lakes. This one has the best setting, with a lush meadow surround and the occasional heron.

Towering in the Woods

As you continue along the track, heading north and back into the woods now, you'll see a peculiar-looking tower peeping out from the canopy of trees. It's 150ft (45m) tall and all that remains of Osmaston Hall. The tower was designed to accommodate all the hall's various chimneys in one single stack. With this odd sight still lingering in your thoughts the walk ends in fine 'lord of the manor' style as you walk down the hall's main drive, saluted by a fine avenue of lime trees.

WALK 48 DIRECTIONS

❶ Turn right out of the Osmanton Village Hall car park and follow the road past the Shoulder of Mutton pub to the village green and duck pond.

Turn left and then take the middle of three rights of way – marked 'Bridleway to Shirley'. The track descends among fields and through attractive woodland. Continue on the track past Home Farm, which lies to the left.

2 Follow the track it as it separates the two narrow lakes, to walk between them.

3 After passing an old watermill keep to the track ahead, which climbs up through the woodlands of Shirley Park. The track eventually becomes a tarmac lane, continuing towards Shirley.

4 The return path to Osmaston, highlighted by a Centenary Way (CW) waymarker, begins on the right, just before the village, but most walkers will want to take a look around the centre, if only for refreshment at the Saracen's Head.

5 Return to the previously mentioned footpath, which begins with some steps. Beyond a stile it crosses a fenced-off section of lawn, previously part of a garden belonging to the cottage on the left. Beyond a second stile the path follows a hedge on the left round the edge of three fields. It cuts diagonally across a fourth field to a stile, beyond which you turn left to descend towards a wood, which is the southern extremity of Shirley Park.

6 Go over the footbridge to cross Shirley Brook and then follow a muddy streamside path to another footbridge. Go over this and then turn right into the woods on a path, which has another CW marker.

7 Beyond a gate at the edge of the woods, ignore the CW path on the right. Instead, leave the woods and continue along a grassy sunken track heading across the pasture ahead and alongside a pleasant lake, the southernmost of the Osmaston Park lakes.

8 Where the track fades, maintain direction alongside the lake and then a narrow strip of woodland. You are walking through the valley of Wyaston Brook and, although the path is invisible on the ground, the stiles in the cross-fences are all in place.

9 The bridleway from Wyaston Grove joins the route just beyond one of these stiles (grid ref 196423). Double-back right along it, passing some railings on the right. The bridleway track now climbs north-east out of the valley and back into the estate of Osmaston Park. It becomes a tarmac drive and eventually turns left on to an avenue of lime trees, emerging by the village green. Turn left, by the duck pond, then right, back to the car park.

Mackworth and Markeaton: a Rural Idyll

Very different from the austerity of the Peak District, this slice of South Derbyshire belongs more to the Midlands than the North.

DISTANCE 6 miles (9.7km) **MINIMUM TIME** 4hrs

ASCENT/GRADIENT 197ft (60m) ▲▲▲ **LEVEL OF DIFFICULTY** ✦✦✦

PATHS Farm tracks and field paths, can be muddy after rain, quite a few stiles

LANDSCAPE Pastoral

SUGGESTED MAP OS Explorer 259 Derby

START / FINISH Grid reference: SK 333379

DOG FRIENDLINESS Dogs can run free in the park away from the playgrounds and along early stretches of riverside path

PARKING Markeaton Park pay car park

PUBLIC TOILETS Markeaton Park

Markeaton Park's a bustling place in summer, but as soon as you cross the road and take the lane up to Markeaton Stones Farm you leave that all behind to enter a new rural world. The farmhouse is pristine, made from that warm-red local brick. The lawns, cottage gardens and stables show further that this place has been cared for.

It was summer when I walked this route, and the track wended its way through fields of wheat that was swaying with the wind and crackling in the heat of the sun. The aura of the place brought Gray's *Elegy* to mind, though the ploughman didn't plod his weary way home, he chugged down the path in his shiny green tractor, just shipped in from Japan.

As you climb the hill towards a stand of trees, look back and see Derby spread before you. Prominent in the view are the university, with its rooftop masts, and the cathedral, which dwarfs everything around it. The beeches of Vicar Wood guide you past the farm of the same name to the other side of the hill, where you can see mile upon mile of rolling farmland. Just beyond some trees lies the landscaped parklands of the estate, down to the hall and All Saints Church. Famous Scottish architect, Robert Adam, built the present hall for Nathanial Curzon in 1759.

A World Apart

A short stretch of road leads to the next cross-field section. Though the walking is a little rougher, it's still pleasantly pastoral. There's a lake in a shady hollow to the right and Bowbridge Fields Farm is a fine 19th-century, three-storey, red-brick building. As you reach the busy A52 there's a brief return to the present day, but Mackworth village is a surprise. It's only yards from the A52, but again, it's a world apart.

A tidy row of 17th- and 18th-century cottages lines an undulating, slightly twisted lane. In the middle is a Gothic stone-built gatehouse, the remains of Mackworth Castle, which was built around 1495 for the de

MACKWORTH

Mackworth family, and destroyed in the Civil War. At the end of the lane is the church of All Saints, a rather austere 14th-century building with a Perpendicular tower. The last mile of the route follows the Bonnie Prince Charlie Walk across fields and back to the civilisation of Markeaton Park.

WALK 49 DIRECTIONS

❶ Leave the car park at Markeaton Park and cross the road to follow a surfaced lane to Markeaton Stones Farm. When you're past the farm the track becomes a stony one, climbing gently around crop growing fields until you reach a T-junction.

❷ Here turn left and then follow a crumbling tarmac lane up past a stand of trees until you reach the buildings of Upper Vicarwood Farm.

❸ At the farm buildings continue through a gate on the left-hand side of the stable block and follow a grassy hilltop track.

❹ Through a gate the track reaches Lodge Lane. Turn left along the lane to the gardens of Meynell Langley, then left again

171

into a field next to the entrance to the drive. The path follows a hedge on the right. Through a small, wooded enclosure a lake appears in a hollow to the right. Beyond the next stile the route enters a large field and the hedge wanders off to the right.

5 Aim for a large lime tree at the far side of the field to locate the next stile. Cross the footbridge spanning Mackworth Brook. The path now goes parallel to a hedge on the right, aiming for a large barn on the hillside ahead.

6 On reaching a gateway the path divides. Take the one to the left, whose direction is highlighted by a waymarking arrow. Go through the next gate and follow the right field edge, passing to

the left of the fine red-bricked Bowbridge Fields Farm. Now head south across fields following a hedge on the left.

7 After going over a stile in a tall hedge, turn left along the pavement of the busy A52 (take care), passing a garage. After 600yds (549m) go left along Jarveys Lane passing through Mackworth village.

8 Where the lane turns sharp right, leave it for a path passing in front of the church. Bonnie Prince Charlie waymarks show the well-defined route eastwards across fields to Markeaton.

9 On reaching the road you can either turn left back to the car park or go straight ahead through Markeaton Park. For the latter go through the gateway, turn left over the twin-arched bridge spanning the lake, left by the children's playground, and left again past the boating lake.

Calke Abbey: the House that Time Forgot

Around Sir John Harpur's forgotten baroque mansion.

DISTANCE *3.75 miles (6km)* MINIMUM TIME *2hrs*

ASCENT/GRADIENT *197ft (60m)* ▲▲▲ LEVEL OF DIFFICULTY ✦✦✦

PATHS *Estate roads and field paths, a few stiles*

LANDSCAPE *Parkland and crop fields*

SUGGESTED MAP *OS Explorer 245 The National Forest*

START / FINISH *Grid reference: SK 352241*

DOG FRIENDLINESS *On lead through farmland and abbey grounds*

PARKING *Village hall car park, Ticknall*

PUBLIC TOILETS *At car park*

Calke is not an abbey at all. The Augustinian order of monks did build one here in 1133 and dedicated it to St Giles, but since 1622 it has been the family home of the Harpurs and Harpur-Crewes.

In 1703 Sir John Harpur had the present Baroque mansion built on the site of the abbey, keeping some of the old 6ft (2m) walls. This was a high society family, but things started to go wrong in the 1790s when Sir Henry Harpur took a lady's maid as his bride. Society shunned the couple and they, in turn, shunned society – the beginning of a tale of eccentricity and reclusiveness that would span two centuries.

Calke was a grand house with many rooms, and here was a family with money. When they tired of one room, they would just leave it the way it stood and move to another. For instance, when Sir Vauncey Harpur Crewe took a bride in 1876, he locked up his bachelor room, along with the heads of stuffed deer he had shot as a youth. When the National Trust bought the house in 1985 they found a dust-laden, neglected, but intriguing place, filled with treasures of centuries gone by.

Ticknall

Ticknall is an interesting village. Passing through it you see some pleasing timber-framed red-brick cottages. When you reach the gates of the abbey, you are confronted with a horseshoe-shaped bridge, arching over the road. Built in 1800, it was part of an old tramway system, which included a tunnel under the main drive to the abbey. Limestone from Ticknall's brickworks used to be carried by horse-drawn trams to the canal at Willesley. On the return journey the load would have been coal. The scheme was abandoned in 1915, now just the bridge remains.

The tree-lined drive sets the scene. There's fallow deer in the woods, as well as barn and tawny owls. Betty's Pond is the first of the several lakes passed on the route. The house, being in a dip, hides until the last moment. Its magnificent three-storey south front includes a four-column Ionic portico. If it's open, it is well worth a visit to see, among others, the Gold Drawing Room and the 18th-century Chinese silk state bed.

CALKE ABBEY

The route heads north to Mere Pond, which is full of lilies and surrounded by attractive mature woods. It reaches its highest point on the fields of White Lees. Here you get glimpses of Staunton Harold Reservoir before you return to Ticknall.

WALK 50 DIRECTIONS

❶ Turn right out of the car park at Ticknall and follow the road to its junction with the A road through the village. Turn left by the Wheel public house, then right by the bridge to go through the

gates of the magnificent Calke Abbey Estate. The tarmac estate road goes between an avenue of mature lime trees and through the Middle Lodge Gates. If you want to go inside the abbey itself you have to pay your entrance fee at the house.

2 Continue south-east along the road, past Betty's Pond (left), then, as the road swings left, carry on along the grassy track to the south end of the park.

3 By a white gate fork left, doubling back towards the abbey, which appears in a dip ahead. After viewing the fine house, continue along the track past the red-brick stables and offices. Cross the grassy, additional car park and follow a path in the top left corner. Go over a stile and down some steps to the Mere Pond, a narrow strip of water surrounded by trees.

4 Turn right to walk along a water's-edge path, then left between the end of the mere and the western extremities of another one, to climb through woodland to the north.

5 On meeting the track at the top edge of the woods, turn left for a few paces, then right through a gate. After tracing the wall on the left, go over a stile in the hedge ahead to enter the next field. The path now heads north of north-west along the left edge of crop fields, passing close to White

> ### WHERE TO EAT AND DRINK
>
> For a bar meal try the Staff of Life on the High Street, Melbourne. There's also a tea room and kiosk at Calke Abbey for paying visitors.

> ### WHAT TO LOOK OUT FOR
>
> By Ticknall's 19th-century church you can see the remains of a medieval church, St Thomas à Becket's, which had become too small. The old church was so strong that it had to be blown up with gunpowder.

Leys Farm. Just past a large ash tree, go over a stile on the left and follow a clear field-edge track ahead through more crop growing fields in the hedge on your right.

6 At a flinted works road turn left, following it through an area of woodland and old gravel pits (now wildlife ponds). The winding track passes several cottages and meets the A514 about 500yds (457m) to the east of the village.

7 Turn left along the road through the village, then turn right, opposite the Wheel pub to get back to the car park.

EXTENDING THE WALK
If you're visiting Calke Abbey while you're in the area, it makes sense to visit neighbouring Melbourne Hall too. You can make an easy extension to this walk, leaving the main route at Point **A** across the fields adjacent to the reservoir before joining the road into Melbourne. Make a little circuit of the town, including Melbourne Hall itself, and return by St Brides Farm and Robin Wood back into Ticknall.

> ### WHILE YOU'RE THERE
>
> Seeing nearby Melbourne is a must. Neat Georgian houses crowd round the Monument in the Market Place. There's a short history of the town engraved on a bronze plaque. The Parish Church of St Michael and St Mary is far grander than you would expect for such a small town. This church, however, was built in the first half of the 12th century for the Bishops of Carlisle, who wanted to be as far away as possible from their troubled border country.

Walking in Safety

All these walks are suitable for any reasonably fit person, but less experienced walkers should try the easier walks first. Route finding is usually straightforward, but you will find that an Ordnance Survey map is a useful addition to the route maps and descriptions.

RISKS

Although each walk here has been researched with a view to minimising the risks to the walkers who follow its route, no walk in the countryside can be considered to be completely free from risk. Walking in the outdoors will always require a degree of common sense and judgement to ensure that it is as safe as possible.

- Be particularly careful on cliff paths and in upland terrain, where the consequences of a slip can be very serious.

- Remember to check tidal conditions before walking on the seashore.

- Some sections of route are by, or cross, busy roads. Take care and remember traffic is a danger even on minor country lanes.

- Be careful around farmyard machinery and livestock, especially if you have children with you.

- Be aware of the consequences of changes in the weather and check the forecast before you set out. Carry spare clothing and a torch if you are walking in the winter months. Remember the weather can change very quickly at any time of the year, and in moorland and heathland areas, mist and fog can make route finding much harder. Don't set out in these conditions unless you are confident of your navigation skills in poor visibility. In summer remember to take account of the heat and sun; wear a hat and carry spare water.

- On walks away from centres of population you should carry a whistle and survival bag. If you do have an accident requiring the emergency services, make a note of your position as accurately as possible and dial 999.

COUNTRYSIDE CODE

- Be safe, plan ahead and follow any signs.

- Leave gates and property as you find them.

- Protect plants and animals and take your litter home.

- Keep dogs under close control.

- Consider other people.

For more information visit www.countrysideaccess.gov.uk/things_to_know/countryside_code